The heyday of steam

The

COLIN WHI

Naval manoeuvres
A *Graphic* illustration of 1890 — typical
the Victorians' romantic idea of the sail

VICTORIA'S NAVY

heyday of steam

KENNETH MASON

End papers
These are of HMS Powerful (1895) armoured cruiser

Cover illustration
The Royal Navy 1885. The confusion in designs is at its height. No two
ships are the same: there are turrets, barbettes and central batteries. In
the foreground, is one of the oddest ships ever built for the Royal
Navy: the 'torpedo ram' HMS Polyphemus (1881). She combined a
vicious ram with the first submerged, side-firing torpedo tubes to be
fitted in a seagoing warship

FOR CHRIS, SUE AND JENNY

ISBN 0-85937-284-7

British Library Cataloguing in Publication Data
White, Colin, *1951—*
    The heyday of steam.
    1. Great Britain. *Royal Navy* — History
    I. Title
    359'.00941   VA454

ISBN 0-85937-284-7

Published by Kenneth Mason, Emsworth, Hampshire

Produced in Great Britain by Articulate Studios, Emsworth
Designed by Sadlergraphics

Contents

INTRODUCTION *page 7*

FROM IRONCLADS TO DREADNOUGHTS *page 8*
The mid-victorian experiments in ship design; the William White
battlefleet; the advent of the dreadnoughts; cruisers; torpedoes; submarines
and aircraft

A BRITISH TAR IS A SOARING SOUL *page 68*
The social changes of the period; daily life afloat; sailors as popular heroes;
training for officers and men and the growth of volunteer reserves

'ROYAL' NAVY *page 99*
The close association of the Royal Family with the Navy — including
Royal Yachts, Fleet Reviews and other royal occasions

SEAPOWER IN ACTION *page 130*
The victorian navy in action — showing the flag; anti-slavery patrols;
exploration; river warfare; sailors ashore. Naval manoeuvres and
the build up to the first world war.

INDEX *page 174*

Introduction

THE HEYDAY OF STEAM 1870-1910 is designed as a companion volume to *The end of the sailing navy 1830-1870* (Mason, 1980). It has the same format; the chapters deal with the same topics; and the index in this volume covers both. Above all, like its predecessor, it deliberately relies for a significant amount of its effect upon the illustrations: all of which come from the collections of the Royal Naval Museum and many of which have not been published before. They are a conscious mixture of photographs, engravings and prints. Purists may prefer photographs only — especially of ships — but the prints and engravings have been included to lend variety and to give a feel for the atmosphere of the period.

Like *The end of the sailing navy,* this is a work of synthesis which draws on the researches and writings of other historians who are more expert than I in their special fields. It is a particular pleasure to be able to pay tribute to the general help and advice I have received from three specialist colleagues: David Brown (ship technology); Nicholas Roger (organisation and decision making); and Kenneth Douglas-Morris (social). However, the technological and social development of the late Victorian and Edwardian navies is a complicated story and so I have been forced to simplify and to cut corners in order to make the final result palatable for the general reader. So, any omissions or errors are my sole responsibility and in no way reflect upon the expertise of these three gentlemen! The last chapter, *Seapower in action* is based entirely on my own researches, since this happens to be my own 'special field'.

I am also glad to be able to acknowledge the support and assistance of a number of friends. At the Royal Naval Museum, the director Ray Parsons has been most understanding and patient about my researches; while I have benefitted greatly from the help of the archivist, Nicola Scadding. Her unique knowledge of the museum's extensive photographic collection has made the task of selecting suitable illustrations immeasurably easier. To the museum's typist, Karen Wakelin, went the unenviable task of converting my scrawl into a workable first draft; while my mother, Margaret White, triumphantly deciphered all my complicated 'second thoughts' to create a final printer's draft. My good friend and fellow-historian Sam Merry has helped, with characteristically honest comments about my historial judgements, at all stages of the operation. And to designer Geoff Sadler MSIAD the book owes its handsome appearance.

'Without them, this book would not have been written', is a much-overworked phrase. In this case, it happens to be true.

All the line engravings come from *The Illustrated London News*. Most of the photographs come from the collection of the Royal Naval Museum, with the following exceptions: pages 98 and 102 come from the Royal Collection and are reproduced by kind permission of Her Majesty the Queen.

Colin S White
Alverstoke Hampshire 1983

Gunnery practice
HMS Iron Duke (1870), Northumberland (1866) and other ships of Admiral Tryon's fleet during the annual manoeuvres of 1890

The sinking of HMS Captain September 7, 1870
Minutes after being hit by a squall off Cape Finisterre, Captain Coles'
revolutionary ironclad lies on her beam ends

EIGHT BELLS HAD JUST STRUCK to herald the arrival of Monday,
September 7, 1870 when the combined British Channel and
Mediterranean squadrons under the command of Admiral Sir
Alexander Milne were hit by a violent squall off Cape Finisterre.
The 10 ironclads, accompanied by a wooden frigate HMS *Bristol*,
had been running northward under sail before a south-westerly
gale, heading home after joint manoeuvres. The weather had
deteriorated fast the previous evening and all the ships were under
double-reefed topsails but, even so, 23 sails were split or blown
away, including four in HMS *Bellerophon* alone. Ten out of the 11
ships heeled under the blow and righted but HMS *Captain* carried
on heeling until she lay on her beam ends. The water poured in
through her funnels and she turned bottom up before plunging
stern first beneath the stormy sea.

It was one of the worst peacetime disasters in the history of the
Royal Navy. Of the *Captain*'s complement of 590, there were only
18 survivors: lost were her Captain, Hugh Burgoyne; Midshipman
Childers, the son of the First Lord of the Admiralty; and her
brilliant though controversial designer, Captain Cowper Coles,
who had been on board as a passenger. The question of whether
turret ships could safely be used as ocean-going vessels had
apparently been answered with a dramatic 'No'.

When the Royal Navy introduced ironclads in 1859 starting with
HMS *Warrior*, she and the other 17 ironclads launched between
1860 and 1865 carried their guns in rows along their gun decks in a
traditional broadside, protected by belts of armour plate. As guns
became more powerful, larger, and heavier, so armour plate was

From ironclads to dreadnoughts

thickened in a search for impenetrability. So fast was this development that, by 1865, no designer could cover the entire length of his ship with armour or equip her with more than a few of the heaviest guns. The age of compromise in ship design had well and truly arrived.

The most revolutionary solution to the problem was that advanced by Captain Cowper Coles during the Crimean war. He had devised a raft called the *Lady Nancy* capable of carrying a 32-pounder gun to within close range of Russian fortifications in the shallows of the Sea of Azoff, in the 1860s, so becoming the leading British exponent of turret-mounted guns. The revolving turret, like so many 19th century innovations, was not the fruit of one man's genius; nor can any one country claim to have been the first fully to develop it. In America, the ideas of John Ericsson led to the building in 1861 of the famous *Monitor,* the first turret ship in action; in France, a similar idea was put forward in the late 1850s by the blind inventor Delaporte but was not adopted and, in Britain, Coles' ideas led eventually to the conversion in 1862-4 of one of the old wooden battleships HMS *Royal Sovereign*. She was capable of operating anywhere in the Channel and, therefore, may be considered as the first sea-going turret ship.

Coles had powerful backers. Prince Albert himself had urged the Admiralty to try out his ideas for a turret ship and the press — notably *The Times* — were vociferously behind him. But the Admiralty remained cautious. After the mid-1860s there was no doubt that turrets offered the most efficient way of mounting and protecting guns. Even under the heaviest fire, Coles' turrets

9

continued to work and to protect their gunners. The question that remained unresolved was could they be fitted in ocean-going ships? Engines were still so inefficient — requiring large amounts of coal and subject to constant breakdowns — that British capital ships, liable to serve all over the world, had to be fitted with full sets of masts and yards which obscured the line of fire from turrets. Moreover, the early armoured turrets were so heavy that they had to be mounted on ships with low freeboard to save weight. But when under sail and heeling to the wind, a high freeboard was needed to provide stability. These limitations, argued the Admiralty backed by their Chief Constructor Edward Reed, meant that an ocean-going turret ship such as Coles proposed was an impossibility. Reluctantly, they at last asked Reed to design a turret ship, but the resulting vessel, HMS *Monarch,* failed to satisfy the Coles camp because her two turrets were placed close together amidships over an armoured central citadel and she had a high freeboard — differing little from her contemporaries in the Black Battlefleet. Under pressure, the Admiralty eventually took the extraordinary step of allowing a ship to be built in a private yard to Coles' design '. . . on the entire responsibility of yourself and Messrs Lairds . . .' (the builders). That ship was the *Captain.*

There were doubts about her from the first. She had a low freeboard but, in a typically exuberant gesture, Coles fitted her with the largest standard sail plan in the Royal Navy — more than 50,000 square feet of canvas — which made Reed concerned for her stability. Moreover, to give his turrets a wider arc of fire, Coles had replaced the lower standing rigging or *shrouds* supporting the

Guns versus armourplate
Throughout the later victorian period, there was a constant drive to produce stouter armour plate and more powerful guns. Shown here, a massive 16.25 inch 110-ton breech loading gun — one of the largest ever made in this period — is tested at Woolwich in 1887

masts with tripod legs — an ingenious solution but one which made the masts too rigid under sail. Most worrying of all, when the ship was loaded with ammunition and stores, her already low freeboard was reduced by another couple of feet to a mere six feet.

Despite these limitations, she passed her sea trials to vindicate Coles' ideas. One doubt remained which was not made public. Her builders calculated that her maximum angle of safety was only 21° (most other warships averaged about 70°) and they suggested that the Admiralty should conduct their own tests. The results, which confirmed the builders' calculations and fears, were sent to the Constructor's office but, before they could be acted upon, the *Captain* had sailed on her last voyage. The combination of turrets, a low freeboard and a full sail plan was never tried again.

Admiralty opposition to Coles' ideas was due partly to caution, partly to the fact that another solution to the problem of combining heavy guns and ever thicker armour in ocean-going ships had been found: the so-called 'central battery'. In this system, favoured by Reed, a few heavy guns were concentrated amidships where they could be surrounded by an armoured box — thus reducing dramatically the expanse of armour needed. The first capital ship so armed was HMS *Bellerophon,* launched in 1865. However, there was no provision for fore-and-aft fire although this defect was partly countered by cutting embrasures in the ship's side to increase the angles of fire (first introduced in the armoured corvette HMS *Penelope,* launched in 1867). Another refinement was the concept of a two-tiered battery which was first used in HMS *Audacious* (1869). In all, 17 central battery ships served in the

Guns versus armourplate
The Prince and Princess of Wales watch the
manufacture of a 14 inch armourplate at Sheffield in 1875

HMS Royal Sovereign (Converted 1862-64)
Designed by Captain Coles and the first sea-going turret ship. Here, she is shown
cleared for action with her bulwarks folded down to give her guns clear arcs of fire

13

Sir Edward Reed
Chief Constructor of the Navy 1863-1870

One solution to the problem of mounting and protecting guns was the turret — a revolving cylinder of armourplate. This idea was developed almost simultaneously in France, America and Britain. In Britain, the main exponent of the turret was Captain Cowper Coles

Interior of an early turret, HMS Glatton (1871)
Note the gun captain in the sighting hatch holding the trigger line. At this time, guns were still individually aimed by their crews

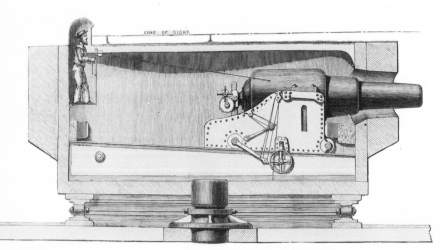

Royal Navy the last of which, HMS *Temeraire*, was launched in 1876 — although she was a hybrid since she combined a central battery with open 'barbettes' fore-and-aft — of which, more later. Perhaps the finest example of the type was HMS *Alexandra* which was launched in 1875 by the Princess of Wales from whom she took her name. She was Mediterranean fleet flagship for more than 12 years — longer than any other ironclad — and a byword for smartness, especially in the late 1880s when painted white on the orders of the Duke of Edinburgh, the C-in-C there at that time.

Like the early turrets, the central battery system had important disadvantages. Despite the embrasured hulls, fore and aft fire was still limited and weight of armament was restricted because there had to be an equal number of guns on each side. Also the large gunports, required to give better arcs of fire, made the batteries vulnerable in action. But, most important, the guns were situated far from their magazines, since the space immediately below the batteries was occupied by boilers and engines. Shells and their charges had to be manhandled along ammunition passages: exhausting and dangerous work. At the bombardment of Alexandria in 1882, an old-fashioned spherical shell penetrated HMS *Alexandra*'s unarmoured stern and came to rest close to where the powder was being handed up. A disaster was averted only by Gunner Israel Harding who, snatching up the shell, doused it in a bucket of water. He was later awarded the VC. A problem remained: turrets gave good arcs of fire but were obstructed by rigging; central batteries enabled full rigging to be fitted but had poor arcs of fire.

HMS Captain (1869)
This view of her stern was taken while she was in dry dock in Chatham just prior to her fatal last voyage. Her very low freeboard is clearly visible

The Monitor and the Merrimac
In 1862 during the American Civil War the early turret ship Monitor (centre)
fought an epic battle with the ironclad Merrimac (left) which demonstrated the
efficiency of the turret

16

17

HMS Monarch (1868) in Grand Harbour, Malta 1882
Reed's version of a turret ship which, largely because of
her high freeboard, proved far more successful than
Coles' Captain

The solution lay in the development of more efficient engines so that masts and yards could be dispensed with and in the early 1870s, this is precisely what happened. The concept of the turret had not been invalidated by the *Captain* disaster: the blame had been placed squarely where it belonged on the excessive sail plan and lack of stability. Turrets continued to be mounted on unrigged coastal defence ships operating only close to their home port. In HMS *Cerberus* and *Magdala* and the four ships of the *Cyclops* class, launched between 1868 and 1871, Reed placed his turrets at either end of a low, central, armoured breastwork with clear arcs of fire fore-and-aft. At the same time, two much larger ships of similar design were laid down: HMS *Devastation* and *Thunderer*, which together with their larger successor, HMS *Dreadnought* (1875), were the basis of battleship design until, in turn, they were replaced by a new type of ship ironically also called HMS *Dreadnought*.

The *Devastation*'s original engines, like those of her contemporaries, were inefficient but her 1,800 tons or so of coal gave her a cruising radius under steam of 4,700 miles as opposed to the *Warrior*'s 1,400 and she was fitted with twin screws which halved her chances of total breakdown. Shortly after her launch in 1871, steamship efficiency was increased by the introduction of the triple expansion engine and cylindrical boilers (the *Devastation*'s steaming radius was doubled when she was fitted with them in 1891). With this, the abandonment of sails in capital ships was possible.

Nonetheless, despite the success of the *Devastation* and, most

Captain Cowper Coles RN
Designer of HMS Captain

19

Central batteries

Another solution to the problem of protecting guns: they were concentrated amidships and surrounded by an iron box. Fore and aft fire was limited and various refinements were introduced to deal with this

particularly the *Dreadnought*, which became known as 'the naval officer's *beau ideal* of a battleship', the 1870s saw no great advances in battleship design. Indeed, between 1872 and 1882, only 10 capital ships were added to the Royal Navy of which four were intended for foreign navies but were bought hurriedly during the 1878 Balkan crisis. The 1870s justly have been labelled 'The dark ages of the victorian navy' and certainly only one striking new design emerged in this period built in response to a similar Italian ship, the *Duilio:* HMS *Inflexible*. She mounted four 16-inch muzzle-loading guns in two turrets amidships — the largest muzzle-loaders ever made — and she was the most famous and prestigious ship of her day. But she marked a step backwards in one important respect since her turrets were mounted amidships with the super-structure fore and aft of them, severely limiting their arcs of fire. At the bombardment of Alexandria, the arcs were found to be even more limited than planned since, when the guns were trained too close to the superstructure, their massive blast shattered the boats mounted there. Nonetheless, her design was considered a success and four smaller versions were ordered: HMS *Ajax, Agamemnon, Colossus* and *Edinburgh*. The last two were the first British ships to mount breech-loading guns since the 1860s.

After experimenting briefly with breech-loaders in the early 1860s, the Navy reverted to muzzle-loaders following a series of accidents involving breech-loaders at the bombardment of Kagoshima during the war with Japan in 1863-4. However muzzle-loading by hand was impractical, guns had become so large that it was even difficult to devise efficient machinery to do the job

20

HMS Hercules (1868)
In an attempt to give some fore and aft fire, Reed designed the Hercules with embrasured ports which increased the arcs of her guns

HMS Bellerophon (1865)
The first central battery ship, designed by Edward Reed. Her port broadside of five
9-inch muzzle-loaders can be seen amidships. But they could not fire fore and aft

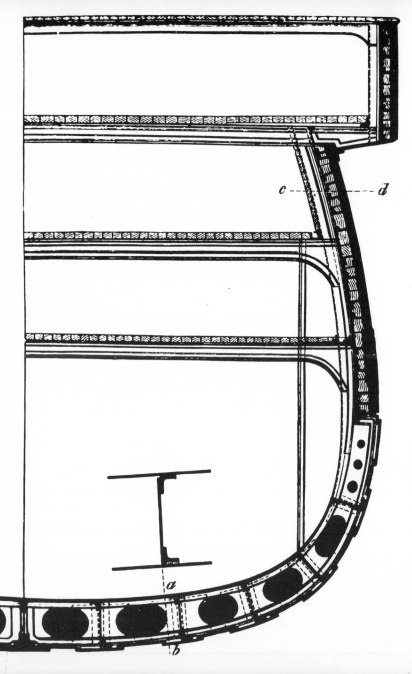

Cutaway plan of HMS Invincible (1869)
Showing her overhanging upper batteries — another
method of giving fore and aft fire

c ----- *d*

— especially when the guns were housed in cramped turrets. In the early turret ships such as HMS *Devastation* and *Inflexible* the loading was done from outside the turrets; between each round, the guns had to be lined up with special loading bays that were housed in the central armoured citadel. Consequently, the rate of fire was ludicrously slow (the *Inflexible* could fire a round only every two minutes) and the method was also potentially dangerous. During live gunnery practice in 1879, the crew of one of HMS *Thunderer*'s guns failed to spot a misfire and operated the loading mechanism, thus double-charging their gun. Fired again, it burst, killing or wounding all in the turret. Such an accident would have been almost impossible with breech-loaders, where the unexploded charge would have been visible as soon as the breech was opened.

By 1880, an interrupted thread method of closing the breech had been introduced making the system safer. At the same time the weight problem posed by the early turrets was solved by the *barbette,* a French gun-mounting consisting of an armoured tower inside the ship which protected the gun machinery and on top of which the guns themselves were mounted on a revolving turntable. In the early examples, the guns were left open to the elements which meant that their crews were exposed to gunfire and to shell splinters. In later models the guns were housed in a protective armoured shield which revolved with the turntable. In their turn these shields came to be known as 'turrets' although they had little in common with Coles' cylinders of armour rotating on rollers.

HMS Sultan (1870)
One of the largest of the central battery ships (9,200 tons),
she mounted 12 heavy guns in a two-tiered battery.
Embrasures and an overhang (seen clearly here) gave
her fore and aft fire

The launch of HMS Alexandra at Chatham, April 7, 1875
The last and the finest of the central battery ships. Instead of embrasures her sides were cut completely away which meant her forward guns could — in theory — fire almost dead ahead. Below is HMS Alexandra's battery, on the lower deck are six ten inch muzzle loaders firing broadside and two firing forward. In her upper battery are four 11-inch muzzle-loaders firing fore and aft

The conning tower of HMS Thunderer (1872)
Sister ship of HMS Devastation. For the first time all the vital controls — steering, engine room telegraphs and voicepipes and voicepipes to the guns — were brought together in one place under armourplate. This was the forerunner of a modern operations room, and below, inside the turret of HMS Thunderer

The lighter weight of the barbettes meant that the *Devastation*'s basic design could be continued in the shape of HMS *Collingwood* (1882). Although the plans themselves were signed by the Director of Naval Construction, Sir Nathaniel Barnaby, who had taken over from Reed in 1870, the new ship was largely the work of his assistant William White, of whom more in due course. Four main factors combined to make the *Collingwood* significant: a top speed of 16 knots, 1½ knots faster than any other capital ship; four 12-inch breech-loaders in barbettes fore-and-aft; a cruising range of 7,000 miles and smaller guns grouped in a battery amidships. So successful was she that the Admiralty ordered a further five ships differing in detail but essentially sister ships: the *Admiral* class. For the first time since the advent of the ironclads, a truly homogeneous fleet was possible.

Even now, there was no drive to modernise and enlarge the fleet. Between 1882 and 1890, only 12 capital ships were launched — low for the world's premier naval power. To understand this lethargy, we must turn briefly to politics.

Although the British Empire was well-established by 1870 the average Briton rarely thought in world terms. Not until the early 1890s did Imperialism become an important political issue when Britain began to see herself as a World, rather than a European, power. The colonial expansion of the 1870s and 1880s was the work of the men on the spot rather than the result of Whitehall policy. Indeed officials on the spot often opposed their political masters — General Gordon for instance who, sent to the Sudan in 1884 to organise the province's evacuation, refused to leave Khartoum

The first mastless battleships

With the development of more efficient engines in the 1870s it was possible for masts and yards to be abandoned. This meant that turrets could again be used to protect the guns

HMS Devastation (1871)
The first British ocean-going mastless battleship. She carried four 12-inch muzzle-loaders in two turrets. The weight of the turrets meant she had to have a low freeboard. This made her very wet in rough seas with the consequence that her guns were difficult to serve

and demanded reinforcements, thus forcing a reluctant government to support him.

Moreover, Britain faced no real threat from her potential rivals on the Continent. France was crushed by Prussia in the war of 1870 and, although the new German empire was proclaimed at Versailles, Germany was not yet seen as a threat, partly because she was a land power with only a small navy and partly because of the ties that existed between the royal families and the ruling classes of both countries. Britain's only serious rival was Russia — indeed, the two countries nearly went to war over the Balkan crisis of 1878 — but her fleet was no match for the Royal Navy. During the 1878 crisis, the Mediterranean fleet sailed confidently up the Dardanelles, as had its predecessor at the outbreak of the Crimean war. Apart from the wave of 'jingoism' which swept the country in 1878 (the phrase originates from a popular song of the time), Britain in the 1870s and early 1880s was blissfully free from the war hysteria that was to be such a feature of 1885 - 1914.

Politically and strategically, then, there was no great pressure for a larger navy which was fortunate as this was a period of confusion in ship design. As we have seen, it was not until 1882 that the Admiralty felt confident enough to order a complete class of ships. Moreover the advent of Whitehead's locomotive torpedo (of which more later) led some naval experts to predict the battleship's imminent demise. No wonder then, that capital ship building slackened so much between 1870 and 1885.

When it came, the change was dramatic. It is usually attributed to a famous series of articles published in 1884 in the Liberal paper *Pall Mall Gazette* entitled 'The Truth About the Navy', although in fact the mood already existed — particularly in informed naval circles. The writer of the articles, W T Stead, obtained many of his facts from disgruntled naval officers — notably Fisher, who was then captain of HMS *Excellent*. Whether the articles created the mood or reflected it, they certainly succeeded in turning the state of the navy into a political issue overnight. The pressure was sufficient to force the Admiralty to draw up a hastily prepared expansion scheme — even in the absence of the First Lord, Lord Northbrook who, significantly, was then in Egypt advising the Khedive on his parlous finances! The scheme envisaged a five-year plan of construction including two first-class battleships, 13 cruisers and 14 torpedo boats; it marked the beginning of intense interest in the navy destined to last until the first world war.

At the same time, the state of Europe altered. France, recovering from the shock of her defeat by Germany, formed an alliance with Russia. The combined navies of the two countries threatened British supremacy in terms of numbers, although the British underestimated the problems of managing two fleets as one unit when there were so many differences in ship design to say nothing of language and objectives. Growing interest in the empire led to a colonial conference in 1887 which raised some disquieting questions about the vulnerability of Britain's overseas possessions and the inadequacy of the obsolete ships guarding the trade routes. Most telling of all, the fleet's efficiency was called into question by the Spithead review held to celebrate the golden jubilee of Queen Victoria in July 1887. Intended as a demonstration of British seapower, naval experts nonetheless were able to recognise the weakness that lay beneath — as, indeed, the main organiser of the review Lord Charles Beresford had always intended they should. 'Most of what you see here is mere ullage,' remarked Admiral Sir William Hewett, referring to the fact that at least one-fifth of the ships on display had been taken from reserve, given a lick of paint and manned with scratch crews to swell numbers. Any foreign observer who had done his homework knew that the effective capital ship strength of the Royal Navy in 1887 was 45, of which 25 had been built before 1870 and were therefore obsolete.

The upsurge of interest in the Royal Navy; the threat from a revitalised French navy in alliance with Russia; a growing awareness that the fleet lacked homogeneity: all these factors contributed in 1888-9 to a call for a greater expansion than that of 1884. A committee was appointed to investigate the state of the service and the qualities of the vessels composing it. Published in early 1888, the report criticised most of the ships and recommended that Britain should maintain a battle fleet equal to the combined fleets of her two most powerful rivals — France and Russia. So began the 'two-power standard' concept which was to dominate naval planning for the next 20 years or so.

In 1889, Parliament passed the Naval Defence Act which provided for the building of eight first class battleships and 42 cruisers supported by the reboilering and rearming of a number of otherwise obsolete vessels such as HMS *Alexandra*, *Hercules* and *Superb*. In charge of this great expansion was William White,

30

HMS Sans Pareil (1887) firing a broadside
Sister ship of the Victoria. The huge guns were so heavy that their muzzles drooped slightly

HMS Inflexible (1876) in Grand Harbour, Malta
The Inflexible mounted four massive 16-inch muzzle loaders, the
largest ever made in two turrets placed en echelon admiships

The experimental designs

Despite the apparent success of the Devastation, the Admiralty continued to experiment with different designs. 1872-1882 was a period of stagnation in ship design and building in Britain and only ten capital ships were launched

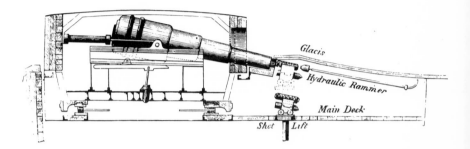

Loading mechanism for HMS Inflexible's guns
After firing, the guns had to be lowered behind an armoured shield to be reloaded. This meant she could fire only one broadside every two minutes

Director of Naval Construction; to him goes the credit for creating the handsome, homogeneous fleet of the late victorian period.

Despite the success of the *Admiral* class, ship design had remained unsettled during the 1880s. Barbettes were felt to be too exposed to the heavier quick-firing guns being developed, so the old-fashioned cylindrical turrets were tried again. The two battleships of the 1884 programme, HMS *Victoria* and *Sans Pareil* were fitted with two huge new 100 ton breech-loaders which, with their stoutly armoured turret, were so heavy that only one turret could be fitted in each ship. Their successors, the *Nile* and *Trafalgar*, which appeared in 1890-1, had low freeboards to compensate for the weight of their turrets and this meant that their guns were awash in heavy seas or when the ship was steaming at full speed.

As White began to work on the ships of the Naval Defence Act, he was enabled to dispense with the low freeboard entirely thanks to the introduction of Harvey steel armour plate. A ship's armour could now be much lighter since six inches of the new plate gave the protection of 10½ inches of the old. By using this new material and by returning to the barbette system of gun mounting, White was able to produce high-freeboard ships with handsome, balanced appearances which, with modification, were the basis of all battleships launched between 1891 and 1905. The 'new look' was heralded by HMS *Royal Sovereign*, the name-ship of a class of seven but it was the next class, the nine *Majestics* which first embodied all the new ideas and which proved the most successful. They were followed by the *Canopus* class (six ships) in the late 1890s; the *Formidable* and *London* class (eight ships) in 1898-1902;

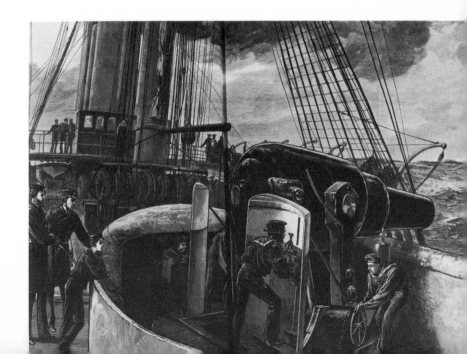

The forward barbette of HMS Temeraire (1876)
The Temeraire was a hybrid. On her main deck, she had six guns in a standard central battery. On her upper deck were two 11-inch guns mounted in barbettes. When fired, the guns recoiled into an armoured pit where they were reloaded

HMS Temeraire (1876)
in Portsmouth Harbour

HMS Benbow (1885)
The aerial view shown left gives a
vivid impression of the layout of
the Admiral class. Unlike her
sisters, the Benbow mounted two
massive 16.25-inch guns

Admiral class battleship
in a seaway
A major defect of the Admiral
class, pictured right, was their
low freeboard which meant that
their guns were awash in
heavy seas

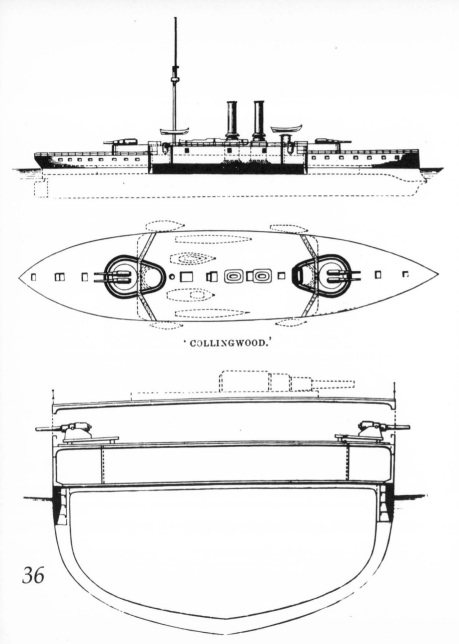

' COLLINGWOOD.'

The first modern battleships

The true forerunner of the late victorian and edwardian battleship was the Admiral class. The first, HMS Collingwood (1882), had a top speed of 16 knots, and a cruising range of 7,000 miles. Her four 12-inch guns were in turrets fore and aft and she had a secondary battery of six six-inch guns amidships. This layout was to be repeated in successive classes until the launch of the Dreadnought in 1906

the *Duncan* class (six ships all launched, remarkably, in 1901) and the most powerful of all, the *King Edward* class (eight ships), launched between 1903 and 1905. With the addition of a further three second class battleships, 48 capital ships were launched in just 14 years — a ship-building programme unparalleled in history.

So, by 1905, Britain possessed its strongest ever peacetime battlefleet made up of modern ships of uniform design capable of operating as fleets — an advantage no rival navy shared, since none had succeeded in settling on a single successful type. Those British fleets were infinitely more efficient than before. Annual manoeuvres, started in 1887, had created a generation of flag officers and captains accustomed to operating together in large units. As we shall see in more detail later, those manoeuvres, together with the day-to-day routines of the fleets, became increasingly realistic under the influence of Sir John Fisher in the Mediterranean; Lord Charles Beresford in the Channel and Sir Arthur Wilson, who earned a reputation as the greatest of Britain's edwardian sea-going admirals. Even the ships themselves looked more warlike for between 1902 and 1905 the splendid victorian livery of black hulls, white superstructures and buff funnels and masts was abandoned for dull neutral grey.

Yet, as this splendid fleet reached its pinnacle of power, so was it threatened. Until the early 1900s, most naval tacticians expected that battles would be fought at close-range — around 1,000 to 2,000 yards — so battleships tended to be armed with heavy quick-firing secondary guns ranged in broadsides along their superstructures to

Farewell to masts and yards
HMS Monarch (1868) left background and Iron
Duke (1870) foreground, the last fully masted capital
ships in active service on their last cruise with the
Channel Squadron in 1890. Inset
HMS Northumberland (1866). Engraving by
W L Wyllie

HMS Royal Sovereign (1891)

The first of the William White battleships. Launched by Queen Victoria (see page 120), and below, HMS Majestic (1895) the first ship armoured with Harvey's steel armour which was much lighter than the old compound variety

The William White battleships

In 1889, the Naval Defence Act provided for eight battleships and 42 cruisers. The Director of Naval Construction was Sir William White who designed ships of handsome balanced appearance. These first generation vessels formed the basis of all capital ship design for the next 15 years

Sir William White
Director of Naval Construction 1885-1902

HMS Resolution (1892)
One of the second batch of the Royal Sovereign class. She is seen here on manoeuvres in 1903

provide maximum firepower. William White's usual combination was four 12-inch guns housed in barbettes fore and aft, with 10 or 12 six-inchers along the sides. Fisher, when Controller of the Navy in 1892, advocated a combination of the smallest large gun and the largest small gun and, in a characteristic gesture, he chose as his flagship in the Mediterranean in 1899, HMS *Renown*, a second class battleship which mounted four 10-inch and 10 six-inch guns.

Around the turn of the century, a number of developments combined to change this view. Cordite, introduced as a propellant in 1889 burned slower and more accurately than the older explosives, so that length and range of guns could be increased. It made little smoke and so, for the first time, gunners could see their targets. Increased ranges were now possible and so accurate range-finding instruments were developed during the middle and late 1890s. By 1900, battle practice was being carried out at much greater ranges than 10 years earlier. Fisher, for example, insisted on ranges of 5500-7000 yards when he held the Mediterranean command 1899-1902. Although single guns could be fired effectively at such distances, and some excellent results were achieved, it was impossible to fire broadsides since no method existed of spotting and controlling the fall of individual shot. So it was that, in 1903, 'Fire Control' evolved, based on experiments in the Channel fleet under Beresford and in the Mediterranean under Sir Compton Domville and his second-in-command Reginald Custance, a notable gunnery expert. 'Director Control' emerged, by which specially trained personnel were stationed aloft — 39

The new fleet
The William White ships gave the late victorian and edwardian fleet a handsome balanced appearance. Here, the fleets taking part in the annual manoeuvres of 1895 practice steam tactics

initially in the old-style 'fighting tops' but later in specially constructed 'directors' equipped with accurate range finders and with instruments which communicated range and fall of shot to guns' crews below.

Now British battleships began to obtain undreamed of results at ranges of 10,000 yards and more. Two important problems soon manifested themselves. By 1904 capital ships had such a variety of calibres of gun — HMS *King Edward VII*, for example, had four 12-inch, four nine point two-inch and 10 six-inch — that accurate broadside spotting was difficult. Moreover, long range battles demanded high speeds to enable the participants to manoeuvre themselves into an advantageous position. This was most strikingly demonstrated at the Battle of Tsushima in 1905, during the Russo-Japanese war, when the much faster Japanese fleet was able to 'cross the T' of its slower Russian opponents twice in the opening half hour of the action. The William White battleships had been designed for speeds of between 18 and 19 knots which was insufficient to give them the edge over their foreign rivals. Quite suddenly, our battlefleet appeared obsolescent.

These problems were appreciated overseas. In 1903, an Italian naval architect, Cuniberti, put forward his solution in the British publication *Jane's Fighting Ships:* a heavily armoured ship with 12 12-inch guns and a speed of 24 knots. The Admiralty, maintaining the traditional policy of not introducing any innovation until forced to by foreign competition, remained uncommitted but, in 1905, Japan laid down two battleships based on Cuniberti's ideas and the news came that America was preparing to follow suit the

The Wobbly Eight
Because of the design of their underwater lines, the King Edward VII class always moved slightly crabwise through the water. Here a squadron of them is seen on manoeuvres in 1906

HMS King Edward VII (1903)
In drydock at Gibraltar. Name-ship of the King Edward VII class of eight ships. The last class of William White battleships

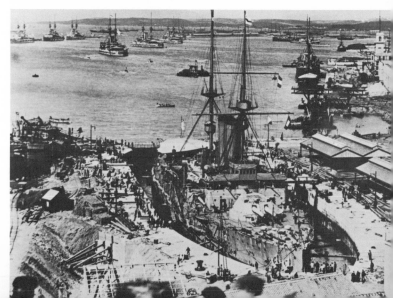

The William White battleships

The Royal Sovereigns and Majestics were followed at regular intervals by a series of similar looking vessels. In all 48 battleships were launched between 1891 and 1905 — a remarkable record

HMS Canopus (1897)
Name-ship of the Canopus class of six ships. The first William White battleship to have her funnels one behind each other

following year. It was time to act. The Constructor, Sir Phillip Watts, who had succeeded White in 1902, was an enthusiastic advocate of the all-big-gun ship with a redoubtable ally in the First Sea Lord — 'Jacky' Fisher. Between them they masterminded a remarkable coup: the British version of the new type of ship, HMS *Dreadnought,* was built from keel-laying to commissioning in one year and a day and was in service by October 1907, two years ahead of her rivals. It was the story of the *Warrior* all over again: Britain had waited for others to make the first move and had then trumped their card decisively. Or so it seemed.

In fact, conditions were very different from those which had existed in 1860. Then, Britain's economic and industrial strength and the weakness of France, had enabled her quickly to establish a commanding lead in ironclads never lost — even in the stagnant days of the 'Dark Ages'. But, by 1900, Britain's industrial lead had disappeared: other countries had caught up with more modern and efficient industries. In Germany, for example, iron and steel production by 1900 almost equalled Britain's, while America's was equal to both. Above all, Britain was failing to adapt to new trends in industry: although almost every new steel-making process originated in Britain, British steelwork owners were reluctant to invest in the new equipment; in electrics and chemicals, where, Britain's scientists had made many of the first advances, America and Germany were the countries which first successfully marketed the final products. To sum up: in 1870, Britain possessed 31.8% or the world's manufacturing capacity (USA 23.33%; Germany 13.2%) by 1910, the percentages were: Britain 14.7%, Germany

43

15.9%, USA 35.5%. Similar downward trends could be seen in Britain's exports and her share of world trade. The prestige and the seemingly inexhaustible new markets and raw materials provided by the empire, disguised the fact that, by 1900, Britain was in economic decline. She still had the capacity to build large and expensive warships and — when driven to it by a Fisher — to build them fast; but she no longer had the capacity to build significantly more ships significantly faster than her rivals.

These facts — the fruit of hindsight and not apparent at the time — have in the past been used to support the argument that the *Dreadnought* should not have been built at all. This, of course, is absurd. Admittedly, her launching placed Britain in a dangerous position since, as we shall see later, she was already locked in deadly rivalry with Germany and the new ship gave the Germans, with their growing industrial capacity, a unique opportunity to catch up. Nonetheless, as we have seen, the all-big-gun battleship was not an exclusively British idea and similar ships were already on the stocks in Japan. Clearly then, there was every advantage to be gained from acting quickly to keep a nose ahead of potential rivals — as Fisher realised. Thanks to his drive, Britain obtained a small early lead which she never lost: the first German 'dreadnought' (as the new ships quickly became called) were not laid down until 1907 by which time the British had one ship in service and three slightly improved ships under construction. By 1910, there were eight dreadnoughts in the Royal Navy as compared with four in the German. All the same, this lead was frighteningly small and provided Germany with a constant

HMS Bellerophon (1907)
A slightly improved version of the Dreadnought. The foremast was
placed forward of the funnel so that the director was not obscured by
smoke and she had a secondary battery of 16 four-inch guns

The coming of the Dreadnoughts

Increases in gunnery ranges and in battle speeds meant that, by 1905, the William White battleships were obsolescent. Thanks to the design of Sir Phillip Watts and the unique drive of 'Jacky' Fisher, Britain managed to have a ship of totally new design, HMS Dreadnought, in service by 1907 — two years ahead of rivals

Sir Phillip Watts
Director of Naval Construction 1902-1912

HMS Neptune (1909)
The first dreadnought with superimposed turrets. This gave her improved fire power astern and on the beam

HMS Lord Nelson (1906)
The last of the pre-dreadnoughts. Designed by Watts with
four 12-inch and ten 9.2-inch

**HMS Dreadnought fitting out in Portsmouth Dockyard and
her launch at Portsmouth on February 10, 1906**
The importance of the new ship was emphasised by the fact that
the ceremony was performed by King Edward VII

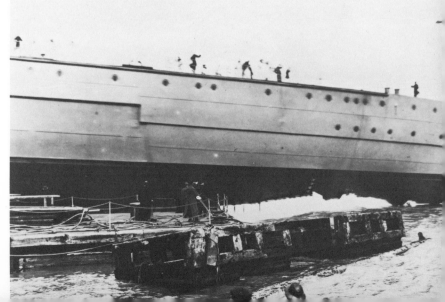

temptation to try to catch up. A vicious arms race ensued, accompanied by periodic public hysteria in both countries that was to prove a contributory factor to the outbreak of the first world war.

The *Dreadnought*, with her great length (527 feet as compared with the 453 feet of the *King Edward VII*); her 10 12-inch guns arranged in centreline and side-mounted turrets so as to give maximum firepower ahead and on the beam; and, above all, her revolutionary turbine propulsion which gave her a top speed of 21 knots, was so successful that she became the basis for all future designs, just as the *Royal Sovereign* had done 15 years earlier. In all, 39 successors were built for the Royal Navy between 1906 and 1944 when the last of the line, HMS *Vanguard*, was launched, of which 31 were commissioned between 1906 and 1916. The *Dreadnought* has often been labelled the most revolutionary warship ever built and certainly, after 1906, naval strength tended to be measured solely in terms of numbers of dreadnoughts. But Britain still

HMS Dreadnought at speed
Like the Warrior before her, the Dreadnought was keenly watched by naval experts. This photograph, taken by a young naval officer, shows her steaming at her top speed of 21 knots

retained a powerful second line in her William White battleships, 27 of which served at sea during the first world war. The *Dreadnought* revolution, drastic though it was, cannot be compared for speed and completeness with that instigated by HMS *Warrior* 50 years earlier.

Cruisers

The dramatic developments in battleship design between 1870 and 1910 were matched by similar changes in the smaller ships of the fleet. In 1870, the word 'cruizer' (so spelt) embraced many types of vessel, from large ironbuilt frigates such as the 5,750 ton HMS *Inconstant* to tiny wooden gunboats. By 1910, the cruiser was a recognised type with various sub-classes, each designed to perform a specific role and, like the battlefleet, homogenous.

Iron came late to smaller ships, partly because of expense and partly because wooden ships were cooler and easier to maintain in tropical waters where so many of them were deployed, defending the empire and on anti-slavery and anti-piracy patrols. Indeed, in the 1860s, a particular type of construction was evolved known as 'composite' in which the strength of an iron framework was combined with the coolness afforded by a wooden skin to provide a compromise vessel that was ideal for service in the tropics. Moreover, masts and yards remained in smaller ships even longer than in the battlefleet, simply because the latter were expected to be within reasonable distance of coal supplies, whereas the former would often spend months at sea on patrol. The first cruisers designed without masts were the *Mersey* class of 1886-7 and the last

to be designed with masts were the six *Cadmus* class ships launched between 1900 and 1903. Most cruising ships of the 1870s were extremely slow — HMS *Shannon*, for example, managed only 12 knots under steam whereas the battleship HMS *Alexandra*, launched the same year, had a top speed of 15 knots. The old difference between the fast, handy frigates which acted as scouts for the lumbering battlefleet in the days of sailing warships had been lost.

The first ships to reverse this trend were HMS *Iris* (1877) and HMS *Mercury*(1878). Designed originally with a light barque rig, they were given powerful engines (7514 horsepower as opposed to only 2590 horsepower in the slightly smaller HMS *Carysfort*, launched in the same year) which gave them speeds of more than 18 knots. Ahead of their time, they were used as 'dispatch vessels' — for example, during the Egyptian crisis of 1882, when the Mediterranean fleet was concentrated off Alexandria, the *Iris* was kept running continually between Alexandria and Malta, carrying messages and supplies.

Once interest in the navy began to revive after 1884, the smaller ships benefitted as much as their larger sisters. The *Iris* and the *Mercury* had been the work of William White who was to have as profound an effect on the development of cruisers as he had on battleships. Indeed, he first made his reputation as a designer of fast, powerful cruisers while employed by Armstrongs, between 1882 and 1885. When he returned to the Admiralty as Director of Naval Construction, a cruiser design which had been put together hurriedly in response to the 'Truth About the Navy' outcry in 1884

50

was already in hand. This was the *Orlando* class, in the balanced appearance of which can be seen the origins of the modern cruiser. A heavy 10-inch waterline belt of armour protected their engines, boiler rooms and magazines but White preferred to incorporate an armoured protective deck in his designs and to do without the belt. The first large cruiser he designed for the Royal Navy with this arrangement of armour was HMS *Blake* (1889). She was followed by nine of these so-called first class protected cruisers which were built between 1890 and 1892 as a result of the Naval Defence Act — all of them around 7-8,000 tons and armed with two nine point two-inch guns and 10 or 12 six-inch guns. Many of them served as flagships on foreign stations: HMS *St George* was the flagship on the Cape of Good Hope station at the time of the bombardment of Zanzibar in 1896 and the Benin campaign of 1897 while, in the same year, the *Crescent* was flagship of the North American station, having succeeded the *Blake* in 1894.

At the same time as the *Orlando*, another smaller but equally successful type of ship was evolved by White with light armour, smaller guns and slightly less speed. The name ship of the class of four was HMS *Mersey* (1885) and she formed the basis of a series of successful cruisers. All were lightly armed; none was larger than 6,000 tons or so and most were capable of about 20 knots. They were known as second class protected cruisers. Some 51 were launched between 1885 and 1902 to form the nucleus of the Royal Navy's worldwide squadrons. During the Boer War there were five of them in South African waters most of which survived to see active service in world war one.

The period 1885-7 also saw the development of a third and even smaller type of cruiser with the introduction of the seven ships of the *Archer* class. Although lightly rigged, with three masts, they were really scaled-down 1770-ton *Orlandos,* carrying six six-inch guns and capable of 14 knots. This type, later known as third class protected cruisers, never exceeded 3,000 tons although, with improved engines, speeds of up to 20 knots were achieved. Again, they were found world-wide, eight of them being present during the Boer war in South African waters.

The evolution of these three types of cruiser meant that the smaller ships of the fleet became a homogenous unit just as the battleships had. And, like the battleships, the smaller ships were affected by the great revolution in design of the early 1900s. The second and third class cruisers merged into one class becoming the so-called light cruisers, the development of which really lies outside our period, because between 1900 and 1908, there was a lull in cruiser building. The experts — especially Fisher — believed that this type of small ship was obsolete and that their duties with the battlefleet could be carried out by the new type of large destroyer then being developed. Obviously, this viewpoint ignored completely the small cruiser's most important function, the defence of trade (always Fisher's blind spot), and the folly of suspending small cruisers altogether was soon realised. In 1903, HMS *Amethyst* had been launched with only four-inch main guns instead of the usual mixture of six-inch and 12-pounders; and turbines which gave her a top speed of 23½ knots. Thanks to a high free-board, she still resembled her predecessors but she was a

The grand fleet
The Third Battlesquadron at Sea c 1914. HMS Conqueror, Monarch and Thunderer (all 1911) seen from the quarterdeck of HMS Orion (1910)

pointer in the right direction. In 1908, when light cruiser building was resumed, the classic modern cruiser lines emerged with HMS *Boadicea*: long, lean and low with four rakish funnels.

So far the ships we have dealt with are logical developments of Nelson's frigates and sloops performing nearly similar functions — in particular, the patrol of trade routes and the defence of colonies. However, during the late 1890s, another type of cruiser began to evolve which certainly had no direct ancestor in the old sailing fleet: the armoured cruiser. To understand how this type developed, we need to retrace our steps.

During the early 1860s, ship designers had assumed that all ships, regardless of size, henceforward would be armoured and, to match the new ironclads, a series of small 3,000 ton ships was launched. The least successful ships, both as fighting machines and as sea-boats, in the entire mid-victorian fleet, they were not repeated. In any case, the increasing weight of armour and guns made it impossible to armour small ships in the same way as capital ships after 1865-6. But the need for protected small ships remained. During the 1870s the Russians decided to plan for a war on Britain's trade by building small, comparatively fast ironclads that could outrun any larger warship and outgun any smaller ship — a combination that proved so successful in the huge American frigates of the 1812 war. The Russian ships were designed to have a long range: for example, the *General Admiral*, launched in 1873, could steam 6,000 miles at 10 knots. Ships such as these posed a threat to Britain's squadrons of lightly gunned, unarmoured cruising ships.

The British tried two answers to this threat. First, they stationed second-class ironclads with the most important colonial squadrons. As a direct reply to the new Russian ships, the ironclads HMS *Audacious* and *Iron Duke* alternated as flagship of the China station in 1872-1889. Although they were powerful enough to deal with the commerce raiders, they were not fast enough to catch them and they were so large that there were few docks in the far east which could accommodate them. The second answer was the development of a partially armoued cruiser which began in 1875 with the launch of HMS *Shannon* and was continued with HMS *Nelson* and *Northampton* (1876), the *Imperieuse* (1883) and *Warspite* (1884). None of these ships was particularly successful; their armouring was patchy, their guns old-fashioned and they were not fast enough to act as cruisers. Indeed they cannot really be considered as cruisers at all; they were second class — and inferior — ironclads. The next design to emerge was the *Orlando* which, with her heavy armament, 19 knots top speed and cruising range of 8,000 miles at 10 knots was at last capable of matching any foreign ship she was likely to meet.

Meanwhile both Russians and French concentrated on commerce-raiding cruisers and their ships grew larger, faster and more heavily armed. White's first class cruisers were criticised, in naval circles, because they were too lightly armed to counter this threat. In the over-excited atmosphere of the time, the qualities of foreign ships tended to be exaggerated and the Admiralty was pressurised to build ships to counter specific foreign designs. In 1895, for example, two massive 14,200 ton first class protected

The masted cruisers

In the 1870s and 80s the word 'cruizer' embraced many different types of vessel, ranging from large, ironbuilt frigates of over 6,000 tons to small gunboats of less than 1,000 tons

cruisers, HMS *Powerful* and *Terrible,* were launched in reply to two proposed Russian cruisers which, when they appeared, were found to be less fast and less heavily armed than had been rumoured. Nonetheless, the craze for armoured cruisers continued and White designed five more classes — a total of 34 ships - before retiring in 1902. In the later vessels, the light armour now available meant that they could be fitted with a belt of waterline armour as well as a protective deck making them more impervious to enemy shell. Herein lay the seeds of a fatal mistake.

As well as being employed on trade routes, frigates and other small ships had always been used as scouts for the battlefleet, although in the Nelsonian period only a small proportion of them had been used in this way. Nelson, for example, had only six small ships with him at Trafalgar. Cruisers had inherited this role but, with the advent of the more heavily armoured classes of the early 1900s, they were given a more aggressive function. Instead of finding the enemy and then staying well out of the way of the ensuing battle, as frigates had done, the new armoured cruisers were envisaged as a fast, mobile wing; strong enough to force its way through a screen of light ships to sight the enemy battlefleet and fast enough to carry out enveloping movements during a battle or to harry a retreating enemy. In 1902, as the first of the new belted and protected cruisers, the *Cressy* class, came into service they were formed into a special cruiser division of the Mediterranean fleet under Sir Baldwin Walker — the first flag officer to command this new type of fighting force. By 1905, there were four cruiser squadrons. The first, second and third were

HMS Calliope (1884)

A corvette of 2,770 tons, mounting four six-inch and 12 five-inch guns. She is famous for having weathered a fierce hurricane in Samoa in 1889, thanks to the excellent seamanship of her crew. Three American and three German warships which were also present sank

HMS Shah

In action with the Peruvian ironclad Huascar May 29 1877

HMS Shah (1873), on the left, was a lightly armoured frigate. She was the first ship to fire a locomotive torpedo in action during her fight with the Huascar

The experimental designs

Masted cruising ships tended to be slow under steam and thus useless as scouts for the
battlefleet. As engines improved during the 1880s, so fast smaller ships were developed. At
the same time, masts and yards were abandoned which meant
that new layouts could be experimented with

made up of the new armoured ships and were attached respectively to the Channel, Home and Atlantic fleets. Only the fourth, made up of older first and second class cruisers, was deployed overseas. Armoured cruisers, their original role as defenders of trade routes now almost forgotten, had become an integral part of the battlefleet.

This trend continued under Watts who, like White, had first made his reputation as a designer of cruisers. He produced three classes, each more powerful than its predecessor, culminating in the three ships of the *Minotaur* class (1906-7) which mounted four nine point two-inch and 10 seven point five-inch guns and had a top speed of 23 knots. Such a mixed main armament, of course, was incompatible with Fisher's ideas and, even as the *Minotaurs* were fitting out, he and Watts were collaborating on another scheme: the development of a dreadnought-style armoured cruiser. And, with the advent of the battleship-cruisers or 'battlecruisers' as they were popularly known, the armoured cruiser fallacy reached its peak.

The old armoured cruisers had been called cruisers, had looked like cruisers and were still regarded as lesser vessels than battleships. The battlecruisers — as their original, fuller name suggests — were seen differently. They looked like dreadnoughts; they were nearly as large as dreadnoughts and they carried the same size, though fewer, guns. During the arms race of 1906-1914, they were counted as dreadnoughts when the relative strengths of the rival navies were assessed. Doubts about their fitness to serve in line of battle were brushed aside: here was an exciting new type

of ship which was going to have an important effect on future battles.

However, there was an important limitation. Battlecruisers were fast — four or five knots faster than the battleships — so that they could force an enemy fleet to action or pursue it. Since weight had to be saved somewhere, they were lightly armoured — the first ship of the type, HMS *Invincible* had only six-inch armour on her sides and a two-and-a-half-inch protective deck as compared with the *Dreadnought*'s 11-inch sides and four-inch deck. Although unable to stand up to the same punishment as a battleship, they came to be regarded simply as fast battleships and with this final, quite logical and understandable step, this unlucky side-development of ship design reached its tragic climax. Nine battlecruisers were present at Jutland, and three of them blew up

54

HMS Imperieuse (1883)
On speed trials in Stokes Bay, before the
removal of her brig rig

HMS Orlando (1886)
The prototype modern cruiser: nine point two-inch guns fore and aft; six-inch guns amidships; no masts; a top speed of 18 knots (forced draught)

The white elephants
In 1895, two large 14,200 ton armoured cruisers, HMS Powerful and Terrible, were launched in reply to two proposed Russian cruisers. At the time they were launched, there was no real use for them. Here, HMS Powerful works up to her top speed of 22 knots

The new cruisers

As a result of the changes in design, the cruisers, like the battleships, became a homogeneous force. There were four distinct types: armoured, 1st, 2nd and 3rd classes

Armoured cruisers — HMS Good Hope (1901)
Used as fast scouting ships for the main battle fleet. The Good Hope was one of the largest of the type: 14,200 tons; two nine point two inch and 16 six-inch guns; top speed 23 knots. Pictured below is the first class cruiser, HMS Endymion (1891). Used mainly as flagships in the overseas squadrons, HMS Endymion was one of the Edgar class: 7,350 tons; two nine point two inch and ten 6-inch guns; top speed 18½ knots

Second class cruisers — HMS Philomel (1890)
The backbone of the overseas squadrons, HMS Philomel was one of the Pallas class: 2.575 tons; eig point seven inch and eight three-pounder guns; top speed 19 knots (forced draught). Inset above is the third class cruiser, HMS Barrosa (1889): 1,580 tons; top speed 16½ knots (forced draught)

The new generation

Small cruiser-building languished between 1900 and 1908 because the experts believed that the type had been made obsolete by the new large destroyers. However, a new type was emerging: the 'light cruiser' of which the forerunner was HMS Amethyst (1903)

HMS Adventure (1904)
Strictly a 'scout' but, like the Amethyst she had one type of gun as her main armament — ten 12-pounders. Also, her low, lean lines foreshadowed the light cruisers of World War One

HMS Defence (1907)
Armoured cruiser building continued under Watts. His last class of this type was the Minotaur class which were heavily armed with four nine point two inch and ten seven point five inch guns

and sank with huge loss of life. Some 35 years later the last of the line HMS *Hood* (1918) went the same way while engaging the *Bismarck* in the Denmark Strait. These disasters destroyed the prestige that the battlecruisers had achieved at the battle of the Falkland Islands in 1914 when, used correctly for the only time in their careers, HMS *Invincible* and *Inflexible* caught and destroyed Admiral Graf Spee's successful commerce-raiding squadron of armoured and protected cruisers.

The battlecruisers were beautiful ships — probably the most beautiful metal ships ever built. But they represented a concept that was dangerously ahead of its time — greyhounds expected to take the punishment of a bulldog. It was only with the fast, powerful battleships of the late 1930s and 1940s that the concept reached fruition. The line of battle was for battleships. Cruisers, however large and however well armed, had no place there.

Underwater warfare

Important though these changes in surface ship design were, more significant developments were in fact taking place beneath the surface. Improved metal working; electrical and diesel propulsion; and more efficient explosives combined eventually to make submerged weapons a real threat.

The first form of underwater warfare to be 'perfected' was the fixed underwater mine or *torpedo* as it was originally called. They were first used in any numbers by the Russians during the Crimean war of 1854-6 but they scored their first successes during the American civil war, when 18 ships were sunk by this type of weapon. Thereafter mines played an increasingly important role,

although it was not until the end of the century that serious thought was given to counter-measures. Minelaying was left in the hands of the Royal Engineers since mines were regarded as part of the country's coast defences until, right at the end of our period, some small cruisers such as HMS *Iphigenia* were converted into minelayers and the supervision of minefields and minesweeping handed to the navy.

The American civil war saw also the reintroduction of an archaic form of warfare at sea which was to affect ship design for almost 40 years. At the same time as the famous *Monitor* was proving the efficiency of the new-fangled turret, her opponent, the *Merrimac*, excited much interest when she rammed and sank two wooden frigates. Four years later, at the battle of Lissa in 1866, the power of the ram was even more dramatically demonstrated when the Austrian ironclad *Ferdinand Max* (powered ironically by engines designed by the inventor of the locomotive torpedo, Robert

Torpedoes — the early days

'Torpedo' was originally a generic term covering all methods of underwater warfare, including fixed mines. Many different forms were tried during the 1860s and 1870s, most of which were either inefficient — or suicidal!

A Spar-Torpedo boat c 1870

The 'torpedo' is an explosive charge in the container at the end of the pole. This can be pivoted until the charge is underwater and extended to its full length. The boat is then driven straight at the target!

Whitehead!) sank the Italian *Re D'Italia* with one blow. For some reason, this return to the classic tactic of gallery warfare was highly attractive to ship designers and large warships in all main navies henceforward carried reinforced bow rams, while a number of smaller warships were designed specifically as 'rams'. So far as the Royal Navy was concerned, the ram proved more deadly to friend than to foe.

More far-reaching (and also first experimented with in the 1860s) was the mobile torpedo of which three basic types emerged. The first was the spar torpedo, in which an explosive charge was attached to the end of a long pole pivotted so that the charge could be lowered underwater. This unwieldy apparatus was mounted in small, fast steam launches manned by a few men. The method of attack was to charge an enemy ship with the spar extended and the charge submerged praying that the launch itself would not be engulfed by the explosion. A second, less suicidal, method was the towed torpedo, invented by Captain John Harvey (and favoured by the young Commander John Fisher, who experimented with it and in 1871 published a detailed manual explaining its use). When an object is towed from the bows of a vessel, it diverges from the ship's course at an angle of about 45°. By attaching an explosive device to a long rope and steering carefully, it was possible to attack an enemy ship without taking one's own ship too close. An inaccurate and inefficient weapon, since the rope often fouled the ship's propellor, it enjoyed brief popularity and, in 1870, was made standard equipment in the Royal Navy for a while.

By then, a more efficient weapon had been developed: the

HMS Thunderer (1872) and torpedo nets

These nets were devised by Captain Arthur, one of the early exponents of the locomotive torpedo, as a counter to all forms of underwater warfare. They were cumbersome and could not be used when the ship was under way

Torpedoes — the threat

The most effective form of underwater weapon proved to be the locomotive
torpedo developed by Whitehead in the 1870s. Various boats and ships designed
for launching them were experimented with

Whitehead locomotive torpedo. Whitehead, an Englishman working for an Austrian firm of marine engineers, secretly developed a prototype built 'in the shape of a dolphin'. With fins to prevent it from rolling it was powered by a small compressed air engine and had a small balance chamber containing a hydrostatic device which controlled the depth at which the torpedo ran — the so-called Secret. Whitehead offered the invention to a number of nations, including Britain. In October 1870, a series of tests were held in the Medway before a committee of naval officers including Captain William Arthur and Lieutenant Arthur Wilson who enthusiastically recommended the new weapon to the Admiralty. The manufacturing rights were bought and the first torpedoes were taken into service early in 1872.

Bearing in mind the stagnation in capital ship building during the 1870s, the torpedo was developed with remarkable speed. To begin with the weapons were carried in launches but, in 1877, the Royal Navy's first specially designed torpedo-boat, HMS *Lightning* was brought into service. All new ships launched after 1872 were fitted with torpedoes and so it was that, as early as 1877, HMS *Shah* became the first ship to fire a torpedo in anger — unsuccessfully as it turned out — during a fight with the Peruvian rebel ironclad *Huascar*. The most significant step came in 1874 when, largely at the instigation of Fisher, a torpedo department was set up as part of HMS *Excellent* in the old wooden frigate HMS *Vernon* which, two years later, became a separate establishment with Captain W Arthur in command and A K Wilson as her commander — a most appropriate reward for the two pioneers. In

A Whitehead torpedo in HMS Active 1890
This is in fact a later model. It is a practice torpedo which has sunk and has been recovered — hence its battered appearance. Left is pictured a torpedo classroom in Hong Kong, c 1900

HMS Hecla (1878) and torpedo boats
The earliest torpedo boats were minute. HMS Hecla was commissioned as a depot ship to carry the boats and all their crews and stores

Torpedo boats stowed in HMS Hecla (1878)
HMS Hecla could carry her boats to within striking range of their target. In this
sense, she was the forerunner of the aircraft carrier

HMS Vernon c. 1890
The torpedo training school HMS Vernon was first set up in 1876. This photograph
shows four ships comprising the school at the turn of the century: (left to right)
Marlborough; Warrior (in background); Ariadne and Donegal

The counter

Various types of ship were tried in an attempt to find and effective counter to the fast torpedo boats. Eventually, in the 1890s, the 'destroyer' emerged

later years Fisher was fond of claiming that he had been responsible single-handed for persuading the Admiralty to adopt Whitehead's torpedo. Although this claim is untrue there can be no doubt that, once he became convinced that Whitehead's invention was superior to Harvey's, Fisher did throw the weight of his personality behind the new weapon to win public approval for it. As to torpedo development, Wilson became the acknowledged expert: he served as commander of HMS *Vernon* from 1876 - 1880, then went to sea as captain of the torpedo boat depot ship HMS *Hecla* between 1881 and 1884, returning to the *Vernon* as her captain between 1889 and 1892. He was promoted to flag rank in 1895 and his first command was a special torpedo squadron formed to test the qualities of the various types of torpedo-carrying vessel then in the fleet. An inventor in his own right, he was largely instrumental in the development of submerged torpedo-tubes in the late 1880s. His most ingenious device was The Pioneer which, when fitted to the head of a torpedo, could shear its way through the wire nets that protected ships.

These nets had been invented by Wilson's companion on the torpedo committee, Captain Arthur, and were first fitted in the armoured cruiser HMS *Northampton* in 1880. They consisted of a skirt of heavy metal netting hung from booms attached to the ship's side. Mounting and stowing these nets was a long, dangerous operation and they could not be used when the ship was under way. So designers turned to the concept of subdividing the hull beneath the waterline into watertight compartments. This had been introduced in the first ironclads but was now approached

in a more scientific manner.

Torpedoes were difficult to perfect. Although the weapons themselves improved steadily as time went by, becoming faster, more accurate and larger with heavier warheads, the ideal method of launching was hard to find. Fitted in existing types of ship torpedoes succeeded only when submerged torpedo tubes were introduced in the early 1890s. Ship's boats were often used, as in the case of the spar torpedo, but these were severely limited in number and size of torpedoes carried. Nonetheless, during the 1880s, this method was popular and a special torpedo boat carrier and depot ship, HMS *Hecla*, joined the fleet to experiment with using the boats against enemy fleets in harbour.

However, it soon became obvious that the best hope lay in developing special torpedo boats. Following the success of HMS *Lightning*, more than 100 boats were launched between 1879 and 1900 ranging from 90ft to 150ft long. Later models were capable of 23 knots in ideal conditions. The French, in particular, developed these craft seeing in them the chance of defeating Britain's classic strategy of close blockade of enemy harbours. Indeed, by the mid-1880s, they were so highly regarded that some experts began to say that the heavy battleship was obsolescent.

True, the torpedo was to sound the death-knell of the battleship — but not for another 50 years. The weapon had to evolve further before it became a serious threat as did the method of launching. Britain began to hold annual manoeuvres in the late 1880s, where the efficiency of the torpedo boats was tested. The boats themselves stood up well to their battering at sea but their crews —

Torpedo gunboats on manoeuvres c 1890
From left to right: HMS Spider, Skipjack and Seagull. This type was ineffective because the ships were not fast enough to catch their intended prey. Their top speed was only 19 knots as compared with the 23 knots of the fastest torpedo boats

exposed as they continually were to the elements — soon became exhausted. The boats could be operated efficiently only close to their home port so, although they made the old close blockades obsolete, they did not influence command of the sea which remained the business of battleships and cruisers. Moreover, the development of machine guns such as the famous Nordenfeldt and Gatling weapons in the 1870s and of quick-firing larger guns in the 1880s meant that the larger ships were able to defend themselves by setting up a wall of fire against which the flimsy boats had no defence.

Nonetheless, the threat they posed to blockading fleets needed an effective counter. Thus, in the 80s, the torpedo gunboat was developed. First of this type was HMS *Rattlesnake,* launched in 1886, but she and her successors were too slow — in fact, in the 1890 manoeuvres, a torpedo gunboat was actually captured by the torpedo boats she was supposed to be hunting! However, with the development of the torpedo boat destroyer, which began with the launch of HMS *Havock* in 1893, the real antidote was found. The *Havock* looked like a large torpedo boat but her extra length and beam enabled her to mount four light guns as well as three torpedo tubes of her own. Her speed of 27 knots made her more than a match for the smaller, slower torpedo boats. So successful did her type become that they replaced the vessels they were supposed to destroy and so, in turn, became the main threat to battleships. And, since they were larger and more seaworthy, they were able to accompany the battlefleets with the result that, by the early 1900s, torpedoes were influencing all aspects of naval warfare and not

HMS Ferret (1893)
One of the first generation of the so-called 'torpedo boat destroyers' from which the destroyer evolved, 280 tons; 195 feet by 19¼ feet; three six-pounder guns; top speed 27 knots

HMS Swift (1907)
Designed as a 'destroyer leader', her armament (four four-inch); speed (36 knots) and general layout made her the forerunner of all modern destroyers

Submarines

Until the development of the locomotive torpedo, submarines had been interesting but impractical oddities. Torpedoes and the development of the periscope turned them into potentially deadly weapons

HM Submarine Holland Three in Portsmouth Harbour
The first type of submarine adopted by the Royal Navy and experimented with in the early 1900s. The officer standing second from left is Lieutenant Charles Little (later Admiral Sir Charles) who in 1901 was the first commanding officer of HMS Dolphin, the submarine base at Fort Blockhouse Gosport. Pictured below is a 'B' Class Submarine (1905) alongside HMS Victory c 1906. 280 tons; 135 feet by 13½ feet; two 18-inch torpedoes; speed c 10 knots

just coastal waters and harbour defence. Their growing threat was yet another factor governing the sudden increase in battle ranges around 1900, which we have already noted. By 1910 'destroyers' as they had become known, were an integral part of the fleet, providing a screen for their own battleships with their high speed and quick-firing guns and waiting always for the chance to attack an enemy battleship with their torpedoes. So large did these destroyer flotillas become that, in 1907, yet another type was introduced: the torpedo boat destroyer leader, the first of which, HMS *Swift*, was 345 feet long, with four four-inch guns and a top speed of 36 knots.

By then, another form of torpedo-launcher had come into its own: the submarine. Before the introduction of underwater torpedo tubes, the submarine had been an interesting but impractical oddity. It could not use its ability to remain invisible for any warlike purpose — apart from spying, and even this could not be done efficiently before the perfection of the periscope in the 1890s.

The torpedo turned the submarine into a deadly weapon. As so often, Britain's rivals first experimented with the concept — most notably, the Americans and French — and, once again, the Admiralty waited until the new weapon had proved itself. In 1900, one of the American models, (known as a Holland craft, after its inventor) was bought and, when proved successful, five similar boats were constructed. In 1904, all five exercised with the Home fleet in special manoeuvres under Sir Arthur Wilson where they triumphantly proved their worth. In his report, Wilson noted how

64

The shape of things to come

By 1910, the first steps were being taken in two fields which were to revolutionise naval warfare: wireless telegraphy and naval aviation. The first successful experiments with wireless at sea were made in 1897 and the first flight from the deck of a British warship was made in 1912

Wireless room in the cruiser HMS Theseus (1892) c 1903

'. . . their presence exercised an extraordinary restraining influence upon the operations of the fleet . . .' and went on to recommend that a special committee should be set up to investigate the best means for dealing with the new threat.

In view of this backing from one of the navy's most influential admirals, the Admiralty decided to proceed further and between 1904 and 1905, the first British-designed class of submarines, the A-class, were launched which, like their predecessors, had a limited range. Thus, during their initial years, submarines tended to be regarded as harbour defence vessels, very like the early torpedo boats. This attitude changed with the introduction in 1905 of the B-class with a range of 1,500 miles and in 1906-7 of the 38 vessels of the C-class. By 1910, the submarine fleet was expanding fast, due largely to the enthusiasm of Fisher who saw the potential of the new idea long before many of his contemporaries and pressed for the building of more submarines even while his attention was occupied with the development of the *Dreadnought*. But not even he was able to forsee how completely the new vessels were to dominate naval warfare in the closing years of the first world war.

Two other important naval branches were also developed in the closing years of our period. Naval experiments with aircraft were begun which led, in 1912, to the formation of the naval wing of the Royal Flying Corps. In December 1911 the first flight was made from a British warship when a Box Kite S27 was launched from a special runway mounted on the fore turret of the battleship HMS *Africa*. Four months later the first launch from a ship under way was made by a Short S38 from the battleship HMS *Hibernia*. Additionally, our period saw the communication of wireless telegraphy. Signal flags were an important method of communication between ships in close proximity — as they have remained to this day — but there was a need for long-distance communication, in view of the ever-increasing battle ranges. The

65

Launch of a seaplane from HMS Hibernia in 1912

problem had been partly solved by one of Wilson's inventions: the truck semaphore, consisting of two large semaphore arms which were fitted to the top of a ship's mast and connected to the signal bridge by a complicated system of levers. By this means messages could be relayed faster and over greater distances than by means of flags. However, in 1896, the first naval wireless transmission was made on board the torpedo school ship at Plymouth, HMS *Defiance*, and, a year later, the telegraphists in the *Defiance* communicated in morse with the gunboat HMS *Scourge* which was under way at distances of up to two miles. Thereafter progress was rapid. The first sea-going, operational wireless transmitters were fitted in HMS *Alexandra, Juno* and *Europa* during the manoeuvres of 1899 and, a year later, wireless was first used on active service at sea when, during the Boer war, ships of a division of the Cape of Good Hope squadron which were blockading the port of Lourenço Marques in an attempt to prevent war supplies from reaching the Boers, were fitted with transmitters. Wireless enabled them to spread themselves over a wider area, while remaining in touch with each other.

Thus by 1910 the Royal Navy had undergone a remarkable transformation. Within the space of 17 years, dreadnoughts, battlecruisers, light cruisers, destroyers and submarines had all been introduced — although, as we have seen, these developments were rooted in the achievements of the previous century and so were the result of continual evolution rather than revolution. Now to look more closely at the men who had lived through that evolution.

A seaplane being hoisted aboard the battleship HMS Hibernia (1905) in 1912

The reserves
The period 1870–1910 saw great expansion of the navy's reserves of skilled men.
The RNR continued to flourish, but the most notable development was the emergence of
volunteer groups: first, the RN Artillery Volunteers (1873–1891) and then
the RN Volunteer Reserve (1903–1958)

A British tar is a soaring soul

THE VICTORIAN AND EDWARDIAN PERIOD was a time of great social as well as technological change. The first steps towards many aspects of modern life we now take for granted — votes for all, universal education, organised hospitals and trade unions — were taken then. Just as the technological revolution ashore was reflected in the Royal Navy, so the new mood of social reform affected the sailor.

Nonetheless, there were few sudden or dramatic social changes in the navy between 1870 and 1910. Indeed, many of the truly startling steps had been taken before then: organised reserves, uniforms, continuous service, regular pay and pensions, medals, improved living condition, ships' libraries, saving schemes, sailors' rests ashore, organised and specialised training; these important aspects of modern life afloat were already well established and had only to be consolidated and further improved.

The problem of maintaining an adequate reserve to man the navy in wartime had been highlighted by the Crimean war fiasco, when elderly coastguards and even Scandinavian sailors plugged gaps in the ships' companies. A proper reserve of merchant seamen had been established and under the energetic leadership of its first Registrar General, Captain J H Brown, the Royal Naval Reserve had flourished, gaining over 16,000 members by 1870. Nonetheless, it was felt that the RNR training was inadequate: they seldom went to sea and had to be content with firing obsolete guns in land batteries. Although, as early as 1869, RNR men had been embarked in active ships for manoeuvres (more than 200 men served in HMS *Agincourt* alone) the experiment was not regularly

69

RNAV marching to Westminster Abbey June 1877
Despite their smart turn-out at occasions such as this, the RNAV tended to be looked down upon as amateurs. Pictured right, RNAV rating stands by his gun while doing sea-time during the annual manoeuvres

A Coastguard (1890)
The original reserve. During the Crimean War (1854-6), elderly coastguards were drafted into the fleet to swell numbers

'Aggie' Weston
Miss Agnes Weston and her devoted helpers did much to soften the rough life of the sailors, both ashore and afloat. Ashore, her main contribution was the setting up of 'Sailor's Rests' where, as this contemporary engraving shows, sailors could obtain good food and a bed

repeated. In 1895 however, two sea-going cruisers HMS *Medea* and *Medusa* replaced hulks as drill ships at Southampton and North Shields and, in 1906, the old system of land batteries and harbour drill ships was abandoned finally. Gunnery had then become too sophisticated for reservists to be used. Instead, they were required to serve aboard sea-going active ships to perfect their seamanship. At the same time, the concept of the reserves was extended by the creation of the Royal Fleet Reserve in 1907 which was designed to retain a pool of recently-retired naval sailors.

In 1875, the office of Admiral Superintendant of Reserves was created, not as a post for men on the point of retirement, but a junior rear-admiral's appointment. As a result, some of the leading flag officers of the late victorian period held it: George Tryon, Edward Seymour, Prince Alfred Duke of Edinburgh, Compton Domville and Gerard Noel, to name the best known. Marks of approval came in 1877 when the Prince of Wales became an honorary captain and in 1908 when, as King Edward VII, he agreed to the creation of the Reserve Decoration for officers' long service and the RNR Long Service and Good Conduct Medal the following year. In 1898, the morale of the reservists had been increased considerably by allowing them to wear naval uniform at all times instead of only when they were embarked in active ships.

The reserves were swelled further by the various volunteer groups formed in this period. As long before as 1853, the RN Coast Volunteers had been founded but their numbers had dwindled and, in 1873, they were abolished. However, the MP for Hastings, Thomas Brassey, a former Civil Lord who maintained a lifelong

RNAV at night gun-drill c 1880

Prizegiving in HMS Warspite 1877
The Princess of Wales on board the privately-owned training ship

interest in the Navy, in 1873 organised the RN Artillery Volunteers, a force mainly concerned with gunnery and drill. It drew much of its support from London and the Admiralty gave it an old gunboat HMS *Rainbow* which was moored on the Thames, close to Somerset House — the berth occupied by RNR drill ships to this day. Despite their enthusiasm, smart turn out at parades, and publicity for the Navy, the volunteers never lived down their 'amateur' image and were never popular with the regular navy. In 1891, a Committee on Reserves recommended that the RNAV should be disbanded.

Nonetheless, the demand for an official volunteer force was still strong and from a committee set up by Fisher in 1902 to investigate the reserves sprang the Royal Naval Volunteer Reserve. Men joining the new force had to agree to serve '. . . anywhere the Admiralty may have been of their services . . .' instead of being confined only to service in home waters as the RNAV had been (in fact, as early as 1879 a RNAV man, R V Jennings, had served ashore in the Zulu War, despite the old limitation). Unlike the RNR, the RNVR had to find their own drill sheds although a generous Admiralty did supply practice guns, rifles and equipment. The force was under the overall command of the Admiral Superintendent of Reserves and its men subject to the Naval Discipline Act. This official recognition made the force far more successful than its predecessor and men of the RNVR were later to serve with distinction in two world wars.

In the regular navy, the humanising trend of the 1830-1870 period continued. Flogging was suspended in peacetime in 1871

Training the men

Systematic training — begun in the 1850s — increased greatly during the period 1870-1910. There were naval training ships at all the major naval ports and a number of privately-run ships

HMS St Vincent c 1880
A First Rate launched in 1815. Converted to a training ship at Portsmouth in 1862. Finally sold in 1906 and the training transferred ashore to Gosport. Below, the mess deck of HMS St Vincent

The Sail Training Squadron 1899
(Left to right) HMS Calypso (1883); Volage (1869); Active (1869) and Ruby
(1876). The squadron lasted until 1899

and in time of war in 1879 — *suspended*, it should be noted, and not abolished. The uniform regulations were gradually altered to provide more practical and simple clothes for both officers and men — although, interestingly, the men still preferred to embellish their uniforms with fancy additions which magically appeared each time they went ashore, such additions made easier by the fact that, until 1907, no ready-made sailor's uniforms were issued. Before then, the men merely received an allowance of cloth. More comfortable messing arrangements resulted from the development of new types of ships in the 1890s and 1900s and, thanks to Fisher, the sailors were provided with knives and forks!

When, in 1904, Fisher began scrapping the many cruisers, he used the men thus released to create the 'nucleus crew' system. By this, the Reserve Fleet was divided into two: the Fleet Reserve and the Dockyard Reserve. The latter needed much work to get them ready for sea, while the Fleet Reserve needed little. The Fleet Reserve ships were manned regularly by a two fifths crew and essential specialist officers — the 'nucleus' if the ship needed to be mobilised in a hurry. Thus large numbers of men were constantly ashore: no longer in wooden hulks in the harbour but, from the early 1900s, in fine new barracks at Portsmouth, Devonport and Chatham.

One interesting feature of the victorian period was the remarkable growth of the temperance movement. Repeated reductions in the navy's rum ration had to some extent controlled drunkenness afloat but 'runs ashore' were still notorious. A temperance society started aboard HMS *Reindeer* in the late 1860s

The loss of HMS Eurydice 24 March 1878
One of the major naval disasters of the victorian period. The training ship HMS Eurydice (1843), was caught in a freak squall off Ventnor, Isle of Wight, and foundered. Only two of her 332 men and boys were saved. The figurehead (right) is now in the Royal Naval Museum. It has a peculiarly appropriate grief-stricken expression

Chaplain and Naval Instructor Rev Frank Stebbing (bearded, standing centre) takes a class of midshipmen in HMS Iron Duke (1870), flagship of the China squadron

led, in 1873, to the formation of the RN Temperance Society helped by a woman known affectionately to generations of sailors as 'Aggie' Weston. A staunch Christian and a strict teetotaller, she began her work among bluejackets by writing to individual sailors about religious matters. Gradually her correspondents increased until, in May 1871, she was forced to print a general letter. She realised that one way to combat drunkenness ashore was to provide the sailors with a place where they could enjoy themselves, without alcohol being available. In 1876, she and her colleague Miss Wintz bought an old grocery store in Fore Street, just outside the main gate of Devonport dockyard, and converted it into a restaurant with reading room attached. This was followed in 1881 by a similar establishment in Portsmouth and, eventually, beds were provided as well. 'Aggie Weston's Sailors Rests', as they became known, were comfortable and friendly places: the volunteer helpers always treated their customers with strict politeness and the buildings were brightly decorated and clean. Some people objected. Agnes Weston's brand of evangelising Christianity occasionally caused offence and she was accused of condescending to the sailors — that meaningless gibe so frequently endured by people of her type. But the sailors, in the main, were appreciative. And her work was acknowledged officially when she was made a Dame of the British Empire in 1918.

The great expansion of the Navy after 1889 meant that there was an ever-increasing demand for trained regular seamen. As a result, the number of boy training ships increased and various new recruiting methods were tried. In 1894, the cruiser HMS

Britannia Royal Naval College, Dartmouth c 1905
The college was transferred ashore from the old hulks in the summer of 1905

Training the officers

As with the men, officers' training was continually expanded both at entry and throughout their careers. Eventually, in 1902, the whole system was revolutionised by the 'Selborne Scheme'. Although named after the First Lord, it was in fact the brain-child of the Second Sea Lord, 'Jacky' Fisher

Northampton sailed round the British coast so successfully that further sail-and-steam cruisers were commissioned for this purpose. Sail training still featured large and was justified mainly as a means of toughening the boys and making them physically dexterous. The Sail Training squadron lasted until 1899 when it was disbanded only because of the manning needs of the Boer War. Training was gradually modernised and old hulks abandoned for custom-built schools: HMS *Ganges* went ashore to Shotley in 1904 and HMS *Britannia* to Dartmouth in 1905 following behind the famous gunnery school, HMS *Excellent*, which went ashore into the new buildings on Whale Island in 1891. Gunnery remained the main subject taught there, but there was a new regime as well: drill. Instead of slouching along in an easy-going fashion as in earlier colonial campaigns, sailors began to march like soldiers. Whale Island 'bull', as this type of precision drill was nicknamed, eventually pervaded the whole service. One has only to compare photographs of crews in, say, 1860 and 1900 to see the effect. In the early shots, officers and men alike are relaxed, informal and often scruffy; by the turn of the century, they have become ramrod stiff, poised and immaculately dressed. The navy had a constant love-hate relationship with Whale Island as is illustrated by a story about George VI: an admiral who had known him when he served in the navy was invited to dinner and asked what he should wear.

'Come in anything but gaiters', was the reply — gaiters being a well-known trademark of the Gunnery School.

Officers' training was also greatly improved. The RN College at

Vice Admiral Sir John Fisher
This photograph was taken when Fisher was C-in-C Mediterranean (1899-1902). As Second Sea Lord (1902-3) he masterminded the Selborne Scheme for officer entry and training. This proved one of the most enduring of his many reforms

The engineering workshop at Osborne College 1905
One of the main features of the Selborne Scheme was that *all* officers were
expected to have a knowledge of engineering

Greenwich opened in 1873 to provide higher university-style education in subjects ranging from pure and applied mathematics to languages and international law. An engineering college was established at Keyham in Plymouth in 1880; independent torpedo schools at Portsmouth in HMS *Vernon* in 1876 and in Devonport in HMS *Defiance* in 1884; a signal school at Portsmouth in 1888; the Royal Corps of Naval Constructors was re-organised in 1883 and a school of telegraphy was established in 1899 in Devonport. These improvements created a new breed of well-trained, broad-minded officers and eased the acceptance of new technology. Even so old-fashioned snobbery still existed and engineer officers, in particular, were patronised. A famous eccentric victorian admiral, Sir Algernon 'Pompo' Heneage took great exception when he discovered that a chief engineer was entitled to the same salute as a captain. He thought for a moment and then cried, 'I haf it!' (he spoke rather affectedly), 'Take away the sentinel's musket!'

To counter this type of attitude Fisher introduced a new education scheme in 1902 when he was Second Sea Lord. *All* new officer entrants were to be trained either at the newly-established college at Osborne on the Isle of Wight or at the new Britannia Royal Naval College at Dartmouth. There they were to study the same subjects and were to specialise only when they reached their early 20s. This scheme attracted more opposition than any other of Fisher's, presumably because it struck at social rather than merely technological roots, but the idea was a success and still forms the basis of officer training today — although the college at Osborne was soon merged with Britannia.

A contrast in style

One new aspect of naval training in the 1880s and 90s was the 'drill' taught at HMS Excellent. This had a marked effect on the appearance of both officers and men. Note the contrast between Captain Fortesque and his officers in HMS Phoebe in 1870 and Admiral May and his officers in HMS King Edward VII in 1905 (below)

One of the less attractive aspects of the period 1904-1910 was the amount of public squabbling between Fisher's faction and those who opposed his ideas led by Lord Charles Beresford. However, Beresford was not an unthinking conservative. During the 1880s he had used his position as MP for Waterford continually to press for new ship designs and social reforms. The lower deck loved 'Jacky' Fisher because of the care he took for their welfare; but they adored 'Charlie B', the hero of a number of dashing exploits both ashore and afloat. In many ways the two men were kindred spirits. And yet they clashed: both were extremely vain, partisan and likely to see any questioner of their ideas as an enemy to crush — and both certainly saw themselves as Saviours of the Navy. When Fisher's term in office as First Sea Lord was specially extended, Beresford (who had hoped for the job himself) took it as a personal attack and, thereafter, waged all-out war on Fisher and his clique — or the 'Fishpond' as it was called. The most ridiculous example of such squabbling was the so-called 'Paintwork versus Gunnery' dispute of 1907. One of Fisher's staunchest supporters, Percy Scott, was then Rear Admiral in command of the First Cruiser Squadron attached to Beresford's Channel fleet. The Kaiser was due to visit the fleet and the ships had to be prepared. However, one of Scott's cruisers, HMS *Roxburgh* asked permission to complete her gunnery practice first. Scott signalled in reply, 'Paintwork appears to be more in demand than gunnery so you had better come in and make yourself look pretty.' A few hours later the rest of the Channel fleet arrived and Beresford made a general signal to paint ship. Four days elapsed. Scott's signal was

An officer's uniforms 1894
This composite picture shows the many different variations of uniform that a late victorian officer could expect to wear. They include: Mess and Ball Dress (third and fourth from left); Tropical (standing centre); and Torpedo Boat Dress (extreme right)

SPECIMEN

The Scott-Beresford feud
One regrettable feature of the period 1905-10 was the feud between those who supported Fisher's reforms and his opponents, led by Lord Charles Beresford (right). One of Fisher's main partisans was the noted gunnery expert and inventor Percy Scott (left)

The sailor in popular art

During the victorian period, sailors were the equivalent of today's pop stars and footballers. They appeared everywhere: in plays, advertisements, popular prints and even in children's games

passed from wardroom to wardroom and embellished until it was seen as a wittily insubordinate *reply* to Beresford's signal. Finally the story reached Beresford himself — and he exploded. Summoning Scott to his flagship, he subjected him to a public reprimand on the quarterdeck without allowing him to reply or explain and then made a general signal to the fleet describing the paintwork signal as . . . 'contemptuous in tone and insubordinate in character . . .'. Finally he wrote to the Admiralty requesting that Scott should be relieved of his command. It was a badly misjudged over-reaction and, worse, it became public. The press seized happily on the story and headlines such as 'Naval Sensation', 'Snappish Sea Dogs' and 'Kaiser Snubbed by British Commander' ensured that a trivial incident developed into a blazing row.

Public concern over this incident serves to highlight the growing interest in naval affairs which was reflected in all areas of daily life. The *Illustrated London News,* almost devoid of any naval interest in the 1870s, became a fascinating source of material on the Navy in the 1880s and after. *The Navy and Army Illustrated* was launched in 1895 with copious photographs of life on board ships and portraits of naval officers in full uniform, accompanied by potted biographies. Sailors were used commonly as advertising aids. The most famous example, of course, was the Player's tobacco advertisement which featured a bluejacket from HMS *Hero* who, when he recognised himself, approached one of his officers who wrote to Players and managed to obtain for him some free cigarettes! Beecham's Pills, Cadbury's Cocoa and Pears Soap all jumped on the naval bandwaggon.

Advertisements
The most famous naval advertisement was the Players sailor, which featured a real-life blue-jacket from HMS Hero. Other companies jumped on the bandwagon

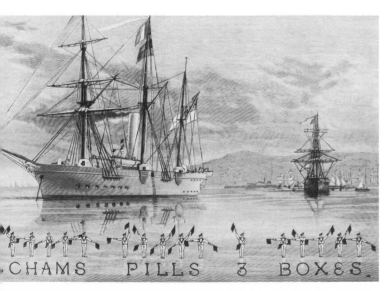

Plays and music

Gilbert and Sullivan's famous opera HMS Pinafore was a parody of the old nautical melodramas. The engraving below shows a special children's performance in the 1880s; the photograph above, a modern production with Little Buttercup selling her wares to the sailors. The music sheet on the previous page reveals how the nautical flavour was introduced everywhere — even into a polka!

So, too, in entertainment. Nautical melodramas of the early victorian period were revived — most notably *Black Ey'd Susan* which had two London productions in 1891 and 1896 and which even appeared at the Avenue Theatre, Sunderland, in 1892 as *Too Lovely Black Ey'd Susan*. Judging by the poster, which combined the death of Nelson with a number of scantily-clad chorus girls, it was a far cry from the original! The old nautical melodramas were guyed in Gilbert and Sullivan's popular light opera *HMS Pinafore* from which the title of this chapter is taken. It was their first big success together and was continually revived. Beresford, a friend of Arthur Sullivan, advised on the correct rigging of the realistic quarterdeck and mast built for the opera. And, in their later opera *Ruddigore,* the character of Richard Dauntless (a sailor who always breaks into a complicated hornpipe at the slightest encouragement), was clearly meant as a joking tribute to the most famous portrayer of sailors of all — Thomas Potter Cooke, who had retired in 1860. These popular entertainments were reflected in more scholarly pursuits. The Navy Records Society started in 1893, thanks largely to the two great naval historians Julian Corbett and John Laughton, has continued to publish high quality works ever since. And, in 1910, was founded the most prestigious of all bodies relating to the study of seafaring — the Society for Nautical Research. Besides organising the restoration of HMS *Victory*, it helped to found the National Maritime and Royal Naval Museums. There were novels and poems by writers such as Kipling, who went twice to sea in a cruiser to experience the atmosphere, and Newbolt. There were parlour games, such as

The Naval Exhibition 1891

The greatest-ever assembly of naval artefacts and memorabilia, the exhibition was opened by the Prince and Princess of Wales

From Sailor Boy to Admiral, a variation on Snakes and Ladders, in which the lucky winner, improbably progresses from a lower-deck boy to an admiral — so long as he avoids pitfalls such as 'A Mutiny' or 'A Riot Ashore'! There were ceramics for the mantelpiece, sailor suits for the children, and innumerable songs and 'nautical arrangements'. In short, the sailor had become a folk hero — the equivalent of today's pop star or footballer.

Public demand for things nautical resulted in the Naval Exhibition, held in the Chelsea Hospital grounds in 1891, the finest collection of naval paintings, memorabilia and ship models ever collected in one place. It is unlikely that it will ever be repeated since many of the items were borrowed from private collections which have long since been dispersed. Stands were set aside also for all the main ship-building, engineering and armaments firms to display their wares. Three exhibits dominated: a full-size working replica of the new Eddystone Lighthouse; the famous field gun run, which still attracts crowds to the Royal Tournament today; and, most impressive of all, a large lake on which two scale 25-foot long models of the battleships HMS *Majestic* and *Edinburgh* fought mock battles. This last was the brain-child of Percy Scott who had sat on the exhibition committee. The models were mounted on ordinary ships' boats, propelled by six men turning crankshafts. The helmsman put his head up through the model pilothouse; the guns were rifles in tubes firing blanks; and a fire was lit under the funnels to create smoke. The exhibition, which lasted for 151 days, was a huge success, attracting half a million people and netting more than £50,000 for naval charities.

The exhibits
Relics of Nelson's life were on show and, pictured right, a pond
on which model warships fought mock battles

Alas, there was another side to the coin. When Henry Capper was promoted warrant gunner, he went to a famous naval tailors on Portsmouth Hard to be fitted for his uniform. All went well until he told the shop assistant his rank whereupon he was directed to another outfitters which dealt exclusively with warrant officers' uniforms. A pamphlet of 1877 tells of how two petty officers tried to buy stall tickets for a music hall in Portsmouth's St Mary's Street, only to be informed that bluejackets were not allowed in that part of the house. While they were arguing with the manager a soldier and a half drunk navvy were let in. Clearly, the sailor's popularity was greatest when he was seen at a distance through rose-tinted spectacles.

Technological and social development were matched by organisational changes. Between 1869 and 1885, three alterations were made in the composition of the Admiralty Board until a well-balanced body emerged which remains almost unaltered to this day. The First Lord was a leading politician who had overall direction of naval policy and responsibility for defending it in Parliament. Under him were four serving naval officers: the First Sea Lord, who dealt with preparation for war and the distribution of the fleet; the Second Sea Lord, who had responsibility for all personnel matters; the Third Sea Lord, whose task was essentially that of the old Controller, in charge of ship-building, ordnance and dockyards and the Fourth Sea Lord, who was in charge of stores and transport. In addition there was a Civil Lord who looked after works and buildings and a Parliamentary Secretary who dealt with finance. Another most important body was the Intelligence Department which was directly accountable to the First Sea Lord. It began in 1882 as the Foreign Intelligence Committee under Captain W H Hall, collecting information about foreign fleets, their ships, manoeuvres and the defences of their ports. In 1887 it became the Naval Intelligence Department with Captain Hall as Director of Naval Intelligence and its scope was expanded to include responsibility for mobilisation and reserves. But the department cast its net far wider than its rather narrow terms of reference dictated. In 1900, for example, it produced a detailed report on the amount of merchandise at stake on the high seas — £523 millions of imports and £534 millions of exports. This timely warning led to increased interest in trade protection and the manoeuvres of ensuing years were designed to test different methods. Once wireless developed, the department worked magnificently in the field of cryptoanalysis and, by 1914, when the famous Room 40 came into existence, most of the German codes had been broken.

As a result of this organised approach to intelligence-gathering, two naval officers, Captains Troubridge and Pakenham, were present as observers in the Japanese fleet when it defeated the Russians so decisively at Tsushima in 1905. Pakenham was on board the Japanese admiral's flagship the *Mikasa*, dressed in full white tropical uniform. A Russian shell exploded nearby killing a number of men and covering Pakenham with blood. To the amusement of the Japanese, he hurried below but their amusement changed to admiration a few minutes later when he reappeared, immaculate again in a fresh white uniform. As for

Troubridge, he later found himself at a dinner on board Kaiser Wilhelm's royal yacht, the *Hohenzollern*. When the Kaiser discovered Troubridge had recently returned from Japan, he asked excitedly, 'What impressions did you derive?' In the midst of an expectant hush, Troubridge replied quietly, 'I only derived one impression from it, sir. The futility of a nation of soldiers taking on a nation of sailors.'

One other story about Pakenham serves well to illustrate the remarkable self confidence of the whole period. In 1908, he was present in Turkey during the Armenian massacres and decided to go ashore to intervene accompanied only by a midshipman and an interpreter. Dressed immaculately as always, he arrived in a village, sat down in a chair in the middle of the square and ordered the frightened midshipman to summon the tribesmen. When a crowd had assembled, Pakenham took out his gold cigarette case, selected a cigarette, lit it and then turned to his interpreter.

'Tell these ugly bastards', he said, 'that I am not going to tolerate any more of their bestial habits'.

88

Living conditions
Despite the social reforms of the victorian period, a large gulf still separated the officers and their men, as is demonstrated by the difference in their quarters

Wardroom, HMS London (1899)

Mess deck, HMS Doris (1896)

Captain's cabin, HMS Majestic (1895)

Daily routine — work
**The victorians' nickname for a sailor was 'The Handyman'.
Certainly, sailors then, as now, had to master many different skills**

Shown below are signalmen hoisting signal flags during annual manoeuvres 1895, and pictured right, painting boats in a battleship on manoeuvres 1896

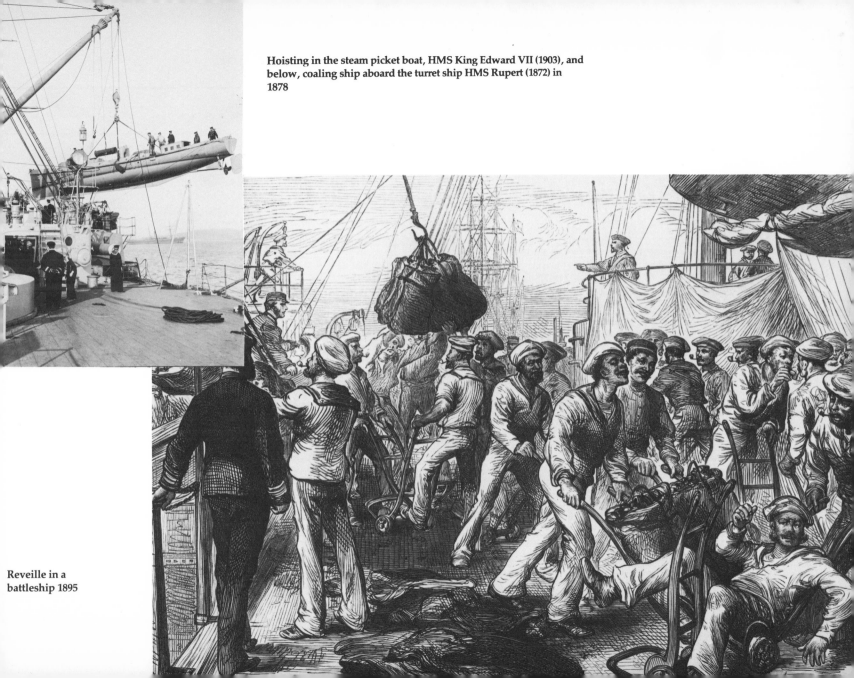

Hoisting in the steam picket boat, HMS King Edward VII (1903), and below, coaling ship aboard the turret ship HMS Rupert (1872) in 1878

Reveille in a battleship 1895

Clearing for action

A much-practiced evolution in the old sailing navy. Once the annual manoeuvre became established in the late 1880s, it became a common feature of life in the late victorian and edwardian navies

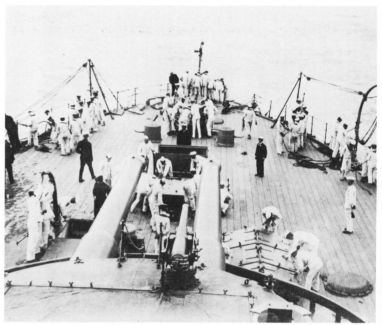

New style
Above and right is shown the quarterdeck of the battleship HMS Irresistible (1898) before and after clearing for action

Old style
The crew of HMS Northumberland (1866), on manoeuvres in 1888, send down topmasts

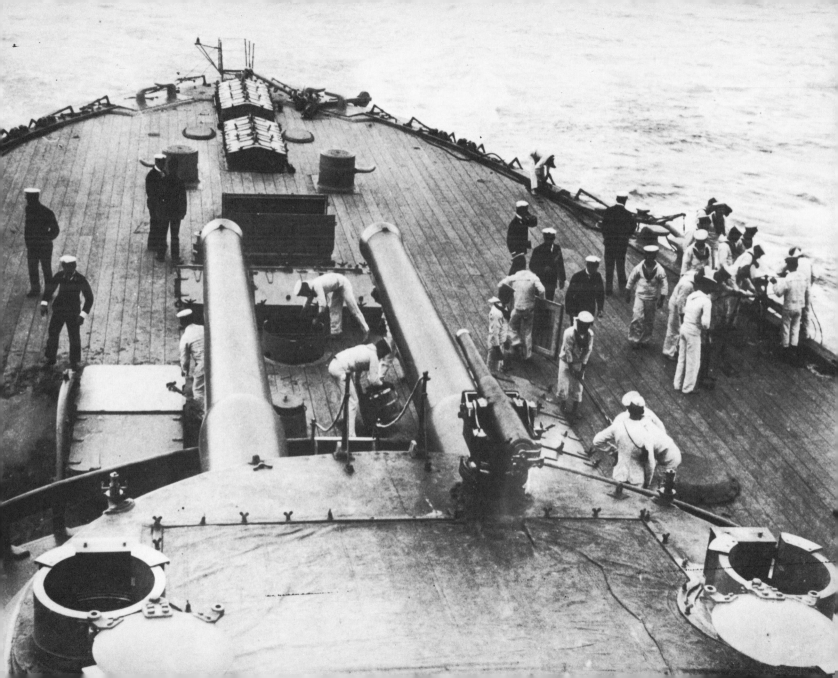

Channel Squadron regatta 1893

Dancing in the armoured cruiser HMS Donegal (1902)

Daily routine — relaxation
Officers' ball on the quarterdeck of a Royal Sovereign
class battleship

An early gramophone in the fo'c'sle of the battleship HMS Duncan (1901)

Christmas decorations in HMS Achilles (1863) — note the ship's cat!

Royal sailors

During the period 1870-1910 royalty were more closely involved with the Navy than at any other time in its history. Three members of the royal family had permanent careers in the service

'Royal' Navy

MEMBERS OF THE BRITISH ROYAL FAMILY have always been adept at reflecting the moods and aspirations of their people but only occasionally have they been trend-setters or trail-blazers. The more remarkable then that in the 1870s, when most Britons were apathetic about their navy, there was a keen interest in the Service among certain leading royals. As a result, when public enthusiasm waxed in the 1880s, the Royal Family were ahead of them encouraging and stimulating renewed appreciation of the navy. Thus it can be fairly said that, between 1870 and 1910, the navy was more truly 'royal' than at any other time in its history.

The main pioneer of this important royal interest was Queen Victoria's second son, Prince Alfred, Duke of Edinburgh, who joined the navy in 1858. Thanks to slightly 'accelerated' promotion in 1866, when allowed to by-pass the rank of commander, by 1870 he was the 26-year-old captain of the 24-gun steam frigate *Galatea*.

The Duke of Edinburgh was one of the most professional of all the royal sailors. Apart from an extended period on half-pay, following his marriage in June, 1874 to the Grand Duchess Marie Alexandrovna, daughter of Tsar Alexander II of Russia, he was on active service almost continuously between 1858 and his retirement in 1893. Appointed to command HMS *Sultan* in 1876, one of the most powerful of the central battery ironclads, he was present when the British Mediterranean fleet steamed up the Dardanelles during the Balkan crisis of 1878. In his ship at that time was Lieutenant Prince Louis of Battenberg, a nephew of the Russian Empress. Somewhat naively, the Duke allowed the young man to invite on board the *Sultan* his brother, Prince Alexander, then serving in the Russian army. The young prince remained for two days, during which he witnessed a number of fleet exercises including the comparatively new-fangled methods for defending battleships against night torpedo attacks.

When news of this apparently innocent visit reached England a first-class 'spy' scandal broke out. It was suggested that Prince Alexander had been shown closely guarded secrets when war between the Russians, with whom he was closely connected, and the British was imminent. A full Admiralty enquiry was demanded and even Queen Victoria — normally quick to defend her family — accused her son of treason. The scandal revived a few months later when the Duke took command of the *Black Prince* in April, 1878, when the *Sultan* went home to refit. The press suggested that the move was intended as a rebuke — although the real motive was to enable the Duke to remain in the Mediterranean instead of returning to England at a time when tension still existed between Russia and Britain and war was still a possibility. Eventually the scandal died down but the story reveals the awkward position in which the inter-connected European royal families often found themselves in times of international crisis: to the Duke of Edinburgh, Prince Alexander was no more than a young relative to whom he wished to be kind; to the British public he was an enemy. History was to repeat itself in 1914, with more tragic results.

The Duke returned to England in the *Black Prince* in late 1878 and on December 30 was made a rear admiral. Since he had served as a captain for 12 years — longer than was then strictly necessary for advancement to flag rank — he had clearly achieved this step on

The Duke of Edinburgh
The Duke of Edinburgh (standing left) as Captain of HMS Sultan in 1878. Next to him is his brother, the Prince of Wales, in the uniform of a Captain RNR

merit. He had received consistently good reports from his superior officers, including a particularly warm commendation from the C-in-C Mediterranean, Lord John Hay, for his organisation of the landing of troops in Cyprus sent from Malta to emphasise Britain's willingness to fight over the Balkan affair.

His first command as a flag officer in 1879 was the Reserve fleet of older first-generation ironclads stationed around Britain, where they acted both as coastguard and reserve drill ships. The main event of each year was a concentration of the ships followed by a cruise which, in 1882, took place just as the Egyptian crisis erupted in June. The Reserve fleet was sent to Gibraltar and ordered to detach its only really serviceable ship, the armoured central battery corvette HMS *Penelope,* and to disembark men to reinforce the Detached squadron, which had been ordered to Malta.

In November 1882, following his promotion to vice admiral, the Duke took over the command of the Channel fleet and then, after a short period ashore in 1885, during which he chaired a committee on pensions for the dependants of seamen, he reached the pinnacle of his career in February 1886 as Commander-in-Chief, Mediterranean. He hoisted his flag in HMS *Alexandra* — by then obsolete with her two-tiered central battery, but still a strikingly handsome ship, a characteristic which the Duke enhanced by having her painted dazzling white. His spell in command was uneventful, but he used the period of comparative peace to restore the efficiency and pride of what was then regarded as Britain's premier fleet — a pride which had been eroded by the constant changes and economies of the 1870s. The distinctive

Famine in Ireland 1881
The Duke of Edinburgh sailed with HMS Lively and Valorous to distribute supplies to the stricken areas. Above, he plans operations in his cabin in the Lively; on the right HMS Valorous distributes food at Kilkerran

Prince Louis of Battenberg
Gatling gun party in Alexandria 1882. As a lieutenant, Prince Louis commanded a Gatling gun ashore during the street fighting that followed the British bombardment of the city on July 11

Mediterranean panache of the 1890s under Tryon and Fisher was very much the Duke's creation.

His last command in 1890 was at Plymouth, upon relinquishment of which in June 1893 he was made an admiral of the fleet. Plymouth was to be his last command for, on August 22, 1893, he succeeded his uncle as Duke of Saxe-Coburg and Gotha and so, as a foreign head of state, had to retire from the Royal Navy, although he retained an honorary rank of admiral of the fleet. He died, suddenly, on July 30, 1900.

The tradition was carried on by two separate branches of his family. His young cousin Prince Louis of Battenburg, a lieutenant in HMS *Sultan* in 1878, was to be a fully profesional naval officer also. He had joined the navy in 1868, becoming a British subject in order to do so, and after a short spell in HMS *Ariadne,* in which the Prince and Princess of Wales were making a cruise in the Mediterranean, he spent four years in the early ironclad HMS *Royal Alfred* on the West Indian station. He suffered from over-friendly relations who, against his will, tried to soften his naval path, as, for example, in 1875, when the Prince of Wales took him in HMS *Serapis* to India. But finally, after spending another 12 months in the Royal Yacht *Osborne* — and turning down a pressing offer to remain even longer — he was appointed in 1880 to the iron frigate HMS *Inconstant,* the flagship of the Detached Squadron which was about to begin an eventful world cruise.

After calling at Montevideo in January 1881, the squadron was diverted to the Cape of Good Hope where the first Boer war had broken out. By the time the squadron arrived the war had ended in

102

Prince Louis as a sub lieutenant

Britain's defeat, so the cruise continued to Australia, Fiji, Japan, China and Singapore. The squadron then turned for home — only to be diverted again, this time to the eastern Mediterranean to take part in a massive concentration of British warships to counter Arabi Pasha's revolt in Egypt (see page 134). On July 11, 1882, the heavy units of the Mediterranean fleet bombarded the forts defending Alexandria where, in the days that followed, riots and looting broke out. Britain had insufficient troops available locally to deal with the insurgents, so seamen and Royal Marines were landed from the British ships — among them the young lieutenant HSH Prince Louis of Battenburg, who commanded a naval detachment armed with gatling machine guns and who thereafter proudly sported the Egyptian campaign medal — the first royal sailor to see action (admittedly, on land!) since William IV, as Prince William Henry, had served in HMS *Prince George* at the Battle of St Vincent a century earlier.

Unlike his cousin, Prince Louis was given no special promotion. A commander in 1885, he served as executive officer in the mastless battleship HMS *Dreadnought* before being given his first command, the torpedo-cruiser HMS *Scout* in 1887. In her he engaged in anti-slaving operations in the Red Sea. In 1891 he was made a captain and after a spell at the Admiralty as adviser to the Second Sea Lord (where he was largely instrumental in the expansion of the Naval Intelligence Division) he was appointed to command the cruiser HMS *Cambrian* in the Mediterranean. He returned to that station again in 1901, this time in command of a splendid new battleship HMS *Implacable* but, before taking over

Dinner to the Kaiser on board the Royal Yacht Victorian and Albert II, 1892
The Kaiser and his host, the Prince of Wales, are seated in the centre background

Review at Spithead 1889
A review held specially in honour of Kaiser Wilhelm. The V and A II, flying the Imperial German Standard at the main is steaming through the lines

104

command, he had been closely involved in Queen Victoria's funeral. The horses drawing the gun-carriage on which the coffin was to be placed became restive after being left standing too long in the biting cold outside Windsor railway station. Prince Louis, seeing that they were unmanageable, suggested that the sailors who were forming the guard of honour at the station should draw the gun-carriage instead — a custom which has been followed ever since at all royal funerals and at the funerals of high-ranking naval officers.

It was while in HMS *Implacable* in the Mediterranean, that Prince Louis first came to the notice of Fisher, his Commander-in-Chief. He followed the great man to the Admiralty in 1902, becoming Director of Naval Intelligence at the same time as Fisher was made Second Sea Lord. He was therefore much involved in the sweeping social and organisational reforms of that period and began to emerge as a truly gifted administrator. Promotion to rear admiral in 1904 began a series of prestigious commands which showed the great esteem in which he was held by the navy: Second cruiser squadron (1904); Second in command, Mediterranean (1907); Atlantic fleet (1908); 3rd and 4th divisions Home fleet (1910). No surprise then, in 1912, when he was appointed First Sea Lord. It was he who issued, on July 18, 1914, the historic signal that sent the British fleet from Spithead (where it had assembled for inspection by the King) steaming at high speed and with doused lights through the Straits of Dover to its war station at Scapa Flow.

And then, at the moment his many gifts were being put to best

Kaiser Wilhelm II of Germany
The Kaiser reviewing a guard of honour of Royal Marine
Artillery at Eastney barracks, 1890

use in a post for which he was so fitted, the blow fell. The British press and public who, 36 years before, had denounced the visit of Prince Louis' brother to HMS *Sultan,* now chose to regard him not as a naturalised Briton, but as a German, and therefore a threat to the country's security. A vicious three-month campaign was directed against him personally as a result of which, on October 28, 1914, he resigned, retired to the Isle of Wight and in 1917, took the title of Marquis of Milford Haven. He died, aged only 65, in 1919.

On the day his resignation was announced, an Osborne Naval College cadet noticed one of his fellows standing on the parade-ground with tears streaming down his face. It was Prince Louis' second son, later to become Earl Mountbatten of Burma and, in his turn, First Sea Lord — the only time the office has been held both by father and son.

It is an ironic quirk of history that in 1914 both Britain and Germany were ruled by men who held high rank in the Royal Navy. Kaiser Wilhelm II in fact had been given the honorary rank of admiral of the fleet, an honour which, at least at the time it was given, he cherished above all others. Always passionately interested in the Royal Navy, it is obvious with hindsight that his obsession with the development of the German fleet stemmed, at least in part, from envy of the splendid naval forces of his British relatives. During the 1890s, as Kaiser, he was a regular visitor to Britain — indeed, in 1901, he actually supported the dying Queen Victoria with his one sound arm — and on every visit he took a keen interest in the latest naval developments. In 1889, the British had even held a special review for him at Spithead.

Welcome home boys
Prince Albert Victor and Prince George of Wales being greeted by their mother Princess Alexandra on their return from a world cruise in HMS Bacchante 1880-1

As for George V, he had fully expected to be a full-time naval officer like his uncle, the Duke of Edinburgh, until the early death of his elder brother, the Duke of Clarence, in 1892, meant that he became heir presumptive. His father, the Prince of Wales (later Edward VII) had always wished to go on active service, like his younger brother Prince Alfred, but Queen Victoria forbade it and he had to content himself with a commission in the RNR. However, he retained an abiding love for the navy, especially once he became King in 1901, for he always took a close personal interest in the many new naval developments that were such a feature of that period.

Bearing in mind the success of his brother's naval career and his own interest in the navy, it is scarcely surprising that the Prince of Wales decided to send his sons to sea at an early age. The two boys joined the service together as cadets in 1877 and, following a spell in the training ship HMS *Britannia*, went on a world cruise in HMS *Bacchante*, a wooden steam corvette which formed part of the Detached Squadron in which Prince Louis of Battenberg served in HMS *Inconstant*. It was during this cruise that the young Prince George acquired a number of tattoos, surely the only British monarch for centuries to have been 'decorated' in this manner!

The elder brother, Prince Eddy (later Duke of Clarence). never served at sea again but Prince George embarked upon a full-scale naval career. Midshipman in the corvette HMS *Canada*, he took courses at the Royal Naval College, Greenwich and HMS *Excellent*, before serving as a lieutenant in the mastless battleship HMS *Thunderer* in the Mediterranean and in her near sister-ship the

The Sailor Prince

Lieutenant HRH Prince George of Wales in command of Torpedo boat 79 during the annual manoeuvres, 1889

Dreadnought. He also spent a short time in the flagship of his uncle, the Duke of Edinburgh, HMS *Alexandra.*

The autumn manoeuvres of 1889 concentrated upon torpedo-boat harassment of an enemy battle fleet in which, despite heavy seas and gales, the little boats rendered sterling service. Among them was TB *79,* commanded by Lieutenant HRH Prince George. The newspaper correspondents who in those carefree days were allowed on board the warships were captivated by the sight of a British prince roughing it with his men. His activities were widely reported — especially when he and his crew narrowly saved a fellow torpedo-boat from wreck after she had broken down at sea in the middle of a storm.

In 1890 he was given his first major command, the gunboat HMS *Thrush* and served in her on the North American station. Then, apparently set for a successful naval career, his elder brother's death destroyed his hopes. Prince George (by now Duke of York) had two more spells in active service afloat: in command of the second-class cruiser HMS *Melampus* in 1892 and of the first-class cruiser HMS *Crescent* in 1898 but otherwise official duties kept him ashore. He never lost his interest in naval affairs and, if the stories told about him are to be believed, he always retained a bluff sailor-like manner like his ancestor, William IV. On one occasion in 1912, when he was inspecting the fleet at Weymouth, the captain of the flagship miscalculated the distance between the foot of his ship's gangway and the gunwhale of the King's barge with the result that King George had to clamber aboard in a most undignified manner. He was furious and, when he returned to the

The fashionable Prince

Prince Albert Edward (Prince of Wales) in the sailor suit made specially for him by the crew of the Royal Yacht in 1846. Taken from the famous painting by Winterhalter

Dressed overall
The Prince and Princess of Wales (later George V and Queen Mary) on board HMS Renown, 1905. Note that the Princess is wearing a sailor's hat!

Royal Yacht, sent for the offending officer.

'. . . When I go for a drive round London they send my carriage round beforehand to see if the bloody wheels go round, and I expect the same thing to be done when I inspect my fleet . . .' he told him. Another indication of his love for the navy is that three of his four sons spent at least some time at sea and one — Prince Albert, later George VI — was present at the Battle of Jutland.

This greatly increased royal interest in the navy was reflected in other areas. For example, the fleet of royal yachts had grown to five by the time Queen Victoria died in 1901. The main yacht remained the *Victoria and Albert II,* a 300 ft paddle steamer, launched in 1855. Prince Albert had been much associated with her design which made her dear to the Queen who grew to dislike change more as she aged. It was customary to retain officers in the yacht for long periods — in one case as long as 14 years — so the Queen became alarmed when she heard that Lord Charles Beresford, then commanding the Royal Yacht *Osborne,* had proposed to the Prince of Wales that service in *that* ship should be reduced to two years. She told Lord Charles that she hoped he would not try to introduce a similar change in the *Victoria and Albert.*

'You may be right' she acknowledged, 'but I am an old woman now, and I like to see faces I know about me, and not to have to begin again with new faces'.

As a result of the Queen's understandable conservatism, a new premier royal yacht was not laid down until 1897 and did not come into full service until after the Queen's death. This was the *Victoria and Albert III* a large, graceful screw yacht with a top speed of 20

The sad homecoming
Queen Victoria's funeral procession, January 1901. The coffin was placed in the deckhouse of the Alberta

HM Yacht Alberta entering Portsmouth Harbour
Launched in 1863 she was used mainly to transport the Royal
Family and their guests between Portsmouth and Cowes when
the Queen was in residence at Osborne House. At 370 tons,
she measured 160 x 20 feet

Royal yachts

By the end of the reign of Queen Victoria, the fleet of royal yachts had
grown to five. They varied in size from larger ocean-going vessels to smaller
craft that were used for short sea excursions

Farewell to power
The Prime Minister, William Gladstone, on board the Alberta in 1892,
en route to tender his resignation to the Queen at the end of his last ministry

...nots (as opposed to her predecessor's 15) and, most important, a ...ruly ocean-going ship. The earlier yacht's trips had all been ...onfined to European coastal waters: visits further abroad, such as ...he Prince of Wales' visit to India in 1875, had to be made in suitable ...N ships. The *V and A III* made many ocean voyages in her long ...nd distinguished career as, like her predecessor, she was in active ...ervice for almost 50 years before she was finally replaced by the ...oyal Yacht *Britannia*.

Besides these larger yachts, there were also smaller ones. HM ...acht *Osborne*, launched in 1868 and displacing 1,850 tons as ...pposed to the *V and A II's* 2,470 tons, was used mainly by the ...rince and Princess of Wales. HM Yacht *Elfin*, a tiny 98-ton paddle ...acht launched in 1849, served to the end of the reign as the ...milk-boat' for Osborne House on the Isle of Wight, carrying the ...ails and supplies from the mainland. But perhaps the most ...ardworking of all the yachts was the 370-ton paddle-steamer ...*lberta*, launched in 1863 and used to convey the Queen and family ...etween the mainland and Cowes and to transport government ...inisters and other important visitors while the Queen was in ...esidence. She also took the Royal Family on short sea excursions. ...onstantly employed in crossing the busy waters of the Solent, it is ...carcely surprising that she was involved in at least one major ...ccident. This occurred in August 1875, when the *Alberta*, with the ...Queen on board, was en route from Cowes to Portsmouth. A ...rivate schooner, *Mistletoe*, began to cross the royal yacht's bows ...nd the yacht's commander, Staff Captain D N Welch altered ...ourse to go under the schooner's stern. Suddenly, the *Mistletoe*

113

HM Yacht Victoria and Albert III
380 x 40 feet, 4,700 tons, launched 1899. A truly ocean-going yacht with luxurious apartments which lasted in service until World War Two, shown here moored next to her predecessor the V and A II at Cowes in 1901

put about and, in an instant, the *Alberta* had run her down, drowning her master and two of her passengers. Although Captain Welch appeared to have acted correctly, the inquest revealed that the *Alberta* had been steaming unusually fast to catch a train at Portsmouth, for which reason the jury failed to arrive at a unanimous verdict.

The *Alberta*'s great moment came towards the end of her career. Queen Victoria died on January 22, 1901, in her beloved Osborne House and, on February 1, the *Alberta* bore her coffin for her last, sad, Solent crossing. Followed by the *Victoria and Albert II* and escorted by eight destroyers, the tiny vessel paddled down a continuous line of battleships and cruisers from Cowes to the entrance of Portsmouth Harbour to the accompaniment of a thunder of minute guns and the wail of boatswain's pipes.

Another striking example of the Royal Family's growing association with the Navy was the increased number of royal visits to dockyards and naval establishments. The Queen slowly emerged from her self-imposed retirement in the 1890s and began to take up again the duties she had performed so enthusiastically until the death of her husband, Prince Albert, in 1861. The great expansions of the navy in the '90s and again in the 1900s were given a seal of approval by the presence of royalty at important launchings — Edward VII both as Prince of Wales and King was particularly energetic. State visits were paid by royalty not only to major countries in the empire such as India, Canada and Australia but also to important strategic possessions such as Gibraltar and Malta. Most striking of all, the number of fleet reviews — usually at

The Royal dining room, Royal Yacht V and A III

114

Visit of the Duke of Connaught to Malta, March 1905
A fine photograph taken by Thomas Barnardiston, Commander of the battleship
HMS Repulse which shows the dramatic effect of the illuminated
Mediterranean fleet and firework display

Royal visits
**After Prince Albert's death in 1861, Queen Victoria largely retired from public life.
However tours abroad and around Britain — such a novel feature of the earlier part
of the reign — were continued by other members of the royal family**

Spithead — multiplied: eight between 1870 and 1901; five between 1901 and 1910, and a further five 1910-14. This made 18 in all; compared with only eight between 1815 and 1870.

These reviews were overtly political. Occasionally, as in 1887, 1897, 1902 and 1910 they celebrated great national events such as a jubilee or a coronation. More often, they were held in honour of — and to impress — visiting heads of state, or to make some point of foreign policy. Thus in 1873 a review was held for the Shah of Persia; in 1886 for visiting Indian princes; in 1889 for Kaiser Wilhelm II of Germany and in 1896 for the founder of the Chinese navy, Li Hung-Chang. In 1878, when war with Russia loomed, when the Mediterranean fleet had already been sent up the Dardanelles and the Channel fleet transferred to the Mediterranean to take its place, a review of 18 major warships was held at Spithead to demonstrate that Britain was still far from defenceless. In 1905, the conclusion of the so-called *Entente Cordiale*

HMS Northumberland (1866)
At sea during the annual manoeuvres in 1888

with France was celebrated by a much-publicised review of the combined French Northern and British Channel squadrons at Spithead. Most striking of all, Fisher's drastic re-deployment of the fleet was demonstrated to the world in August 1907 by the assembly of 172 warships at Spithead — more even than at the 1897 Jubilee and 1902 Coronation Reviews when large numbers of obsolete vessels had been mobilised to swell numbers.

Press and public, alarmed by scares about the state of the Navy and excited by the growing campaign for a larger fleet, reacted to these impressive demonstrations with unparalleled fervour. At each review, the fleet on show was compared — always favourably — with its predecessor.

'. . . The smaller muster of warships could have knocked Sir Charles Napier's squadron (of 1854) into a cocked hat . . .' said the *Hampshire Telegraph* in 1878.

'. . . The difference between an ordinary man of war of today and that of 30 years ago is as great, or even greater than that which distinguishes Sir George Wilkes' flagship, HMS *Inflexible,* from one of the Roman galleys by which our shores were invaded in the days of the illustrious Caesar, . . .' claimed the *Portsmouth Evening News* in 1887. Such claims were understandable, given the bewildering speed with which warships were changing at this time. But overlying these sentiments were others which were even more intoxicating and infinitely more dangerous.

'. . . The fleet thus displayed would be a match for all the navies of the world . . .' (*The Times,* 1873).

'. . . Nine leagues of solid and superb seapower . . . magnificent,

Visit of the Prince of Wales to India, 1875
The Prince on the bridge of the Royal Yacht Osborne
as she steams through the Suez Canal

The christening of HMS Royal Sovereign, February 26, 1891
Queen Victoria inaugurates Sir William White's great expansion of the navy
by christening the first ship of the new design. The ship was 'floated out' at
Portsmouth and not launched in the traditional fashion

Royal launchings

Another striking example of the royal family's growing association with the
Navy was the increased number of visits to dockyards and naval
establishments. Queen Victoria and King Edward VII were present at a
number of launchings of important ships

imposing and nobly imperial beyond all power of description . . .'
(*Portsmouth Evening News*, 1897).

'. . . It is inspiring to reflect that there can scarcely be an hour in
the day when the ceremony of colours so symbolical and so
significant, is not being performed in some part of the world . . .'
(*The Times*, 1902).

British dreams of world-wide influence under the Pax
Britannica combined with seapower, so vividly portrayed in these
magnificently splendid reviews, were rationalised by the rueful
remark of an American naval officer as he watched the sun glinting
on the yellow, white and black paintwork of 165 British warships at
Spithead in 1897.

'I guess, sir,' he said to his host according to the approving
Times, 'This makes for peace.'

Just how tragically wrong that judgment was, we shall see in the
next chapter.

HMS Royal Arthur after her launch; February 26, 1891
The Queen launched the cruiser Royal Arthur on the same day as the Royal Sovereign. The scene was
captured by the young W L Wyllie, then an artist for the Graphic

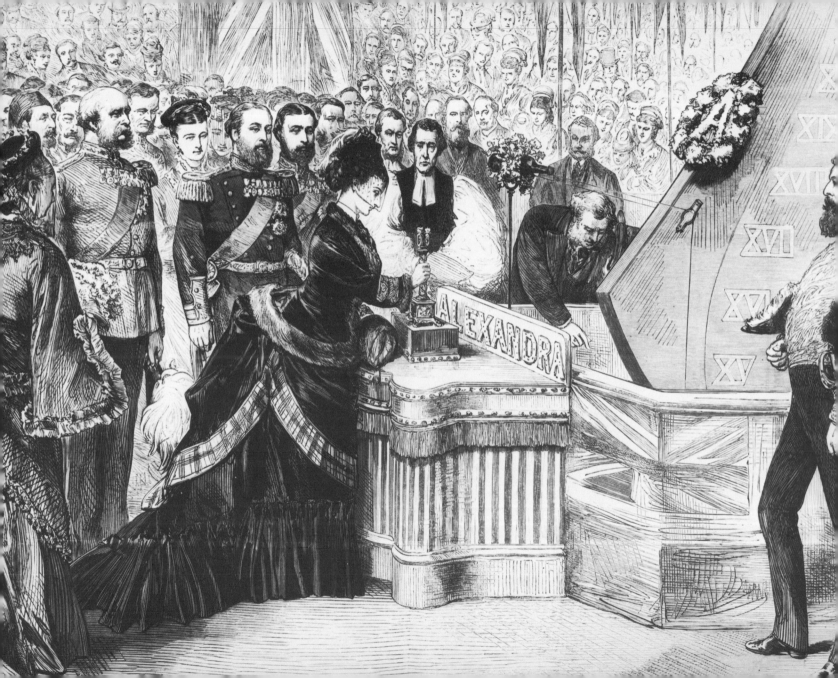

The launch of HMS Alexandra, April 7, 1875
The Princess of Wales, after whom the ship
was named, performs the ceremony

Royal reviews

Between 1870 and 1914, there were 18 major fleet reviews compared with
just eight between 1815 and 1870. As masts and yards died out, the
spectacular ceremony of 'manning ship' had to be changed. Instead of
standing on the yards, the men simply stood around the ships' sides

Review in honour of the Shah of Persia June 20, 1873 (left)

Review of the Particular Service Squadron, August 13, 1878
This was at the height of the Balkan crisis. Note the early torpedo boats. The Queen is accompanied by the Prince of Wales and his family

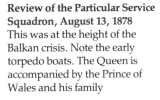

Dinner to the French Officers in the Old Naval Academy, Portsmouth Naval Base 1891
The Academy's dining room is still used as an officers' mess today

The Diamond Jubilee Review June 26, 1897
This stylised view gives a good impression of the sheer size of the fleet of 165
ships that was assembled — without any ships being
withdrawn from a foreign station

127

128

The photographer princess

A number of members of the royal family took an early interest in photography—among them, Queen Alexandra. She passed her interest on to her daughter, Princess Victoria, shown left, in the Royal Yacht V and A III loading her camera

Photograph taken by Princess Victoria of the V and A III entering Malta, April 21, 1909

Showing the flag

In 1870, 91 of the 113 ships in full commission were stationed overseas. The navy was still regarded as a mobile police force, capable of arriving speedily at the source of any trouble

A naval party hoists the Union flag in Guatemala 1874

ON JULY 19, 1870, WAR BROKE OUT between France and Prussia. The superbly organised Prussian army swept all before it and, less than a month later, the Germans had penetrated 150 miles into France; the Emperor Napoleon III had been captured, and Paris was under threat of seige. By January 1871, Paris had fallen and the new German empire had been proclaimed in the Hall of Mirrors at the Palace of Versailles. One of the swiftest victories in the history of warfare, it established Germany as a leading European power. And yet, throughout the conflict, Britain remained neutral. When the Germans attempted a similar coup 44 years later at the outset of the first world war they found themselves fighting British as well as French troops. The story of this remarkable transformation of policy is the theme of this chapter.

The Royal Navy in 1870 was still predominantly an imperial peace-keeping force. Some 113 fighting ships were in commission of which only 22 were concentrated on home waters (including most of the first-class ironclads); of the rest, there were 17 ships in North American waters; 21 in the China and East India squadrons and 12 in the Pacific. Significantly, 11 ships were on detached duty — five of them in the so-called Flying Squadron which was on a world-wide flag-showing cruise. This extended deployment of ships was typical of the mid-victorian approach. The empire was still expanding and, as it did so, Britain's small supply of regular troops became more and more stretched. It was simply impossible to keep large permanent garrisons in all the British possessions and so the Royal Navy was regarded as a mobile police force

Seapower in action

capable of arriving speedily at the scene of any trouble.

This image was also coloured by the altruistic tasks which the navy performed. Hydrography remained an important commitment and, as late as 1900, there were 10 small vessels, two captains, four commanders and about 30 lieutenants and sub-lieutenants employed exclusively in surveying and chartmaking. Exploration, which had occupied the energies and resources of the Royal Navy almost without pause between 1815 and 1859, dwindled in importance after the extraordinary series of Arctic expeditions sent in the 1850s to discover what had befallen the great explorer Franklin. The prime reason was probably that there were no enthusiasts of the calibre of such as Beaufort, Parry, Franklin, Ross and McLintock who had dominated the earlier victorian period. There were, however, three notable achievements in our period. In 1872, HMS *Challenger* was sent on her famous world voyage. A steam-assisted, fully rigged corvette, converted into a floating laboratory she took with her, besides her naval complement of 240, a team of six scientists — including a photographer! She steamed nearly 70,000 miles, collected specimens from land and the depths of the sea and carried out, for really the first time, a systematic and scientific examination of the ocean bed. Commanding for most of the voyage was Captain George Nares who, in 1875, was recalled to England to take command of the first naval Arctic expedition since McLintock had returned in 1859 with the last pathetic relics of Franklin's party. Although this new expedition was primarily scientific, Nares was ordered to go as far north as possible needlessly wasting energy and effort in an attempt to beat the latitude record of 82° 45′N set by Edward Parry in 1827. On May 12, 1876, Commander Albert Markham of HMS *Alert* reached 83° 20′26″ — within 400 miles of the North Pole — but by now scurvy had hit the expeditionary force and Nares was forced to return home early.

There followed another lull in polar exploration until the turn of the century when Scott and Shackleton focussed attention on the Antarctic. As in the Arctic expedition of 1875-6, the desire to reach the pole seemed to over-ride scientific aims and, in the case of Scott's second expedition of 1910-12, lead to tragedy. For having reached the South Pole on January 17, 1912 only to find that a rival Norwegian expedition under Amundsen had managed to arrive there first, Scott and his four companions died on the return journey.

Another altruistic task performed by the Royal Navy was the suppression of slavery and piracy. The West African slave trade across the Atlantic had dwindled almost to nothing by 1870 thanks largely to the continual patrols of the British West Africa squadron who knew the points of departure and the likely destinations of the slavers. Captains of patrolling vessels could plan the movements of their ships in the sure knowledge that certain routes were likely to be used by slavers. On the east coast the points of departure were more numerous, and possible routes more complicated, so that patrols were more difficult to plan. One tactic was for a patrol vessel to cruise off a stretch of coast, dropping boats at all the principal anchorages to establish depots. These boats then carried out their own patrols and were regularly supplied by the mother

131

The Flying Squadron passing Diamond Rock, Martinique in 1871
A specially-formed squadron of wooden sail and steam frigates and corvettes which undertook a world-wide flag-showing cruise

ship. Thus, while in the west of Africa the typical anti-slaving operation usually entailed speedy chases for many hundreds of miles with long-range gunnery; in the east, the operations were usually far fiercer, bloodier, hand-to-hand affairs between small boats' crews and the crews of the swift Arab *dhows* which were used by the slave traders.

The British also tried to stop the slave-trading at source either by treaty with local chiefs or by direct annexation of territory. Inevitably, clashes ensued, invariably involving naval forces as they could be easily deployed. Indeed, between 1885 and 1900, there was scarcely a year when naval personnel were not fighting somewhere on the African east coast. In 1896, for example, there was trouble in Zanzibar, a notorious slaving centre. The anglophile Sultan died on August 25 and his throne was seized by a usurper inimical to the British. Sailors were landed from HMS *Philomel* and *Thrush*, luckily in harbour then, to defend the British Agency. For two days naval reinforcements arrived until by August 27, five ships were assembled including the first class cruiser HMS *St George*, flagship of Rear Admiral Harry Rawson who was C-in-C of the Cape of Good Hope squadron. All British women and children were evacuated to the ships and an ultimatum delivered. At 9 am on August 27 the squadron opened fire; 37 minutes later the usurping Sultan's flag was lowered and by midday the rightful Sultan had been proclaimed. It was a classic example of swift and decisive use of seapower.

Indeed, during the late victorian period, seapower was often used successfully to achieve British political aims — sometimes 133

The British East Indies Squadron in the Mozambique Channel 1890
Vice Admiral Sir Edmund Fremantle leads the ships of his squadron into African waters

without a shot being fired. In 1878 war broke out between Turkey and Russia whose troops advanced on Constantinople. British foreign policy insisted that Russia should be allowed no Mediterranean outlet so, inevitably, Disraeli's Government felt obliged to intervene. The Mediterranean fleet under one of the great victorian admirals, Geoffrey Phipps Hornby, was sent up the Bosphorus, braving mines and heavily-armed forts on the way, and reached Constantinople just before the Russian army. The Russians, believing erroneously that the ships were crowded with troops and unwilling to become embroiled in a war with Britain and other European nations, halted their advance without a single British gun being fired in anger. The fleet remained off Constantinople while a long drawn out peace conference deliberated in Berlin. At times, the negotiations appeared about to collapse so, to strengthen the hand of the British delegation, the Channel fleet was dispatched to the Mediterranean. In a deadly game of chess their threat was used with skill and moral courage to avert a war.

Four years later similar methods were used less successfully, when the Egyptian crisis erupted. The opening of the Suez Canal in 1869 involved Britain and France, the principal European shareholders, in keeping the peace in the Middle East and thus in the internal affairs of Egypt, by then almost bankrupt. In 1881 a mutiny in the Egyptian army led by Colonel Arabi Pasha threatened the already unstable regime of Khedive Tewfik whereupon Britain and France felt obliged to intervene.

Britain assembled units of the Mediterranean fleet off

The voyage of the Challenger

In 1872, the corvette HMS Challenger (1858) was sent on a world voyage of exploration and hydrography. Commanded by Captain George Nares, she steamed nearly 70,000 miles and carried out a systematic and scientific examination of the ocean bed

The drag net used to collect specimens from the sea bed

Sailors of HMS Challenger emptying the drag net

Alexandria under Vice Admiral Beauchamp Seymour. The build-up was supposed to be a joint Franco-British exercise but the French, concerned about conflict, sought ways to withdraw. When war seemed likely, the Channel Squadron, reinforced by ships and men of the First Reserve Squadron, was sent into the Mediterranean; a world cruise by the Detached Squadron was cut short and it too deployed to join Seymour; while ships of the East Indies Squadron were assembled in the Red Sea. When the deployment began on May 12, there had been just six ironclads and an assortment of smaller ships in the Mediterranean. By mid-July 35 ships had been gathered from points as far apart as Trincomalee and Devonport and concentrated in the eastern Mediterranean and Red Sea alone. As the only communication between the Admiralty and its forces was land-based telegraph, this concentration was remarkably swift.

Sadly, however, it did not achieve its aim. Despite repeated warnings and ultimatums, Arabi's men continued to rearm the Alexandrian forts and there were violent anti-foreigner demonstrations. Finally, Seymour was ordered to bombard the forts and to restore order to the town. So it was that a fleet of mid-victorian ironclads fired their guns in anger for the only time in their history. The ensuing bombardment provides some fascinating insights into the efficiency of ships which, as we have seen, were on the point of being superseded by the new designs of the late 1880's and 1890's. British gunnery was extremely accurate although, admittedly, the range was short — no more than 1,000 yards in some cases. Despite this close range and despite the fact

HMS Challenger off Cape Challenger on Kerguelen Island

HMS Discovery is fitted out in Portsmouth dockyard
The Discovery was a wooden storeship which was bought in 1874 and converted into an exploration ship

Cutting up ice for fresh water in the Arctic

that the Egyptians had more than 40 modern rifled guns, the ship's armourplate provided excellent protection. But some weaknesses were also revealed. We have already noted on page 14 the major problems caused in the central battery ships by the distance between magazine and gun. In HMS *Inflexible*, then considered the finest ship of her day, delays in serving her muzzle-loading guns with corresponding pauses between broadsides, led her captain, 'Jacky' Fisher, to suggest that she should be lengthened to enable a secondary battery of lighter, quick-firing guns to be mounted — an interesting recommendation in the light of his later obsession with all-big-gun ships. British fuses were found to be faulty, as was most strikingly shown after the bombardment when an unexploded shell was found lying in the middle of a fort's magazine. Organisational weaknesses of the fleet were also demonstrated. The Egyptians put up a most spirited resistance, so that the bombardment lasted for much longer than expected and, as a result, most of the ships were very short of ammunition by the day's end. Fortuitously the supply ship, *Humber*, arrived in the middle of the battle and saved the day but no proper provision for replenishment of vital stores had been made. Once the lessons of the battle had been analysed, the first steps towards director control were made by installing voice pipes between the gun batteries and the fighting tops since, quite by chance, a number of captains had noted in their reports that, in the heat and smoke of battle, sighting reports from the tops had been more accurate than those from the deck. A seemingly obvious concept emerged only as the result of actual experience — almost accidentally.

HMS Discovery among the icebergs

Captain Robert Scott RN CVO

Scott of the Antarctic

Scott led two important expeditions to the Antarctic. In the second (1910-12), he managed to reach the South Pole but found that the Norwegian, Amundsen, had reached there first. Scott and all his companions perished on the return journey

The bombardment was a tactical success and the Egyptians were forced to withdraw from their badly damaged forts, but then a flaw in the British plans showed. There were no troops available to take possession of the abandoned forts and city or to pursue the retreating enemy. Arabi's men were able to take up strongly fortified positions to the south and a full-scale army had to be transported to Egypt to dislodge them. Seapower had failed to avert the crisis in the first place and now, used inefficiently, it had failed, on its own, to end the crisis.

Seventeen years later, in 1899, it worked superbly. At the outbreak of the second Boer war there was much sympathy in France and Russia for the Boers' plight. In October, when war broke out, the French Mediterranean fleet cruised to the Levant, where it was ideally placed for a junction with the Russian fleet. The British response was immediate: on October 7 part of the Reserve fleet had been mobilised, which meant that the Admiralty felt confident enough on October 13 to move the entire Channel fleet — eight modern battleships, two armoured cruisers and four small cruisers — to Gibraltar. A *Globe* correspondent with them described the warlike precautions: extra sentries by night; men sleeping at their guns with ammunition ready to hand on deck. Thereafter, as the troop transports left Southampton, they were escorted past the French coast by the reinforced Channel fleet cleared for action. The French continued to cause alarm by their apparently warlike preparations and, in March 1900, Russia even proposed a three-power intervention with France and Germany. Anglophobia mounted, especially in Germany, when the British

Scott's ship, the Terra Nova, in the ice during his last expedition

imposed a total naval blockade of Delagoa Bay to prevent war supplies from reaching the Boers. But this was sabre-rattling. As a Berlin newspaper commented, '. . . Even if England sends 100,000 men out to South Africa, she will be in no wise weakened as regards Germany; since, in this case, only the fleet comes into serious consideration and England continues to have her navy entirely at her disposal . . .'. In 1912 a loyalist member of the South African Parliament summed up the situation thus, '. . . It was Britain's absolute command of the sea during the Anglo-Boer war of 1899-1902 that assured her success . . . who will deny that a great naval war was fought out in certain foreign cabinets from which the seapower of Great Britain emerged triumphant . . .'. Despite the serious reverses which Britain suffered in South Africa and a long drawn out costly war, seapower limited the conflict to the African continent.

Nonetheless, the *Pax Britannica* was only a relative peace: there were no major wars, it is true, but there were numerous small-scale campaigns usually over local questions of sovereignty within the British empire. And because, as we have seen, the local garrisons were always small, sailors and Royal Marines often found themselves fighting alongside them.

Boatwork was the skill which sailors could bring to these campaigns, for which there was a long tradition stretching back into the eighteenth century. In the early victorian period, this had been used on the rivers of China and, in the 1880s and 1890s, it was continued in Africa. Earlier, ships' boats had been used but, in Africa, custom-built river steamers were more common. For

139

The fight against slavery

Although the west African slave trade had been largely stamped out by 1870, the trade in the east continued. A constant battle against the slavers was maintained by British ships in those waters

example, between 1889 and 1893 there was continual trouble with slaving chiefs around Lake Nyassa and the River Zambezi. Two Yarrow-built prefabricated stern-wheel steamers, HMS *Herald* and *Mosquito* were transported to East Africa. They were involved in a number of incidents, not always with humans. On one patrol, the *Mosquito* was attacked by a hippopotamus which put its head through her bottom and filled the breadroom.

'. . . These unwieldy brutes are always doing something unpleasant to boats . . .' commented her commanding officer. The two steamers were so successful that, in 1893, the Admiralty ordered a further three, the *Dove*, *Adventure* and *Pioneer*, for service on Lake Nyassa itself. The Rivers Zambezi and Shiré which connected the lake to the sea were impassable in certain places so the two steamers had an unusual journey. They were shipped in pieces to the mouth of Zambezi, arriving in October, 1892, where they were taken in lighters 300 miles upriver to the River Shiré rapids. There they were loaded onto wagons and manhandled to the shores of the lake. On May 30, 1893, the *Dove* was launched and the two other boats followed within a few days. The *Adventure* and *Pioneer* were used extensively in 1893 and 1894 against troublesome tribes in the area and were so successful that both their commanders received the CMG in 1895. By this time, however, the Admiralty had handed the boats over to the administration of British Central Africa and the Royal Navy ceased to be involved on Lake Nyassa.

These small-scale campaigns were repeated, in various forms, all over Africa during the late victorian period, but the most

The bombardment of Zanzibar, August 27, 1896
Zanzibar was a notorious slaving centre and the British tried always to maintain control there. In 1876, in pursuance of this policy, ships of the Cape of Good Hope Squadron under Sir Harry Rawson (right) bombarded Zanzibar and the Sultan's palace (below)

An attack on a slaving dhow, 1892
This print shows vividly the fierce, bloody, hand-to-hand fights which were such a feature of the fight against slavery in this area

Seapower in action

Seapower was often used during the victorian period to achieve British political aims. Sometimes, it was not necessary for a single shot to be fired

striking use of naval personnel in river work was seen on the greatest African river of all: the River Nile. Once embroiled in Egyptian affairs in 1882, the British found it difficult to extricate themselves and they also became increasingly involved in the vast Egyptian dependency of the Sudan. In 1883 a religious leader called the Mahdi began a religous war against the Egyptian overlords and their British allies. His operations were so successful that, in 1884, the British government decided on an evacuation of the Sudan and General Charles Gordon was sent to Khartoum to organise it. Exceeding his instructions, Gordon remained in Khartoum concerting resistance to the Mahdi whose force had begun to seize control of all the Sudan, including that part to the north of Khartoum through which Gordon would have to retreat. A relief force had to be sent to link up with or even rescue Gordon. Despite the many rapids which made the river impassable to all but the smallest boats, the force commander, Sir Garnet Wolseley, was strongly in favour of an advance directly up the Nile valley. Having successfully used river transport in the so-called 'Red River' campaign in Canada in 1870 he was convinced that similar methods could be re-used. Some 377 Canadian boatmen (or *voyageurs* as they were called) were engaged and 800 flat-bottomed whale boats ordered, together with a number of steamers to pull them. Sailors assisted in the transport of the relief force on the river itself and a naval brigade of about 150 officers and men under the command of Captain Lord Charles Beresford marched with the force and played an important part in the fighting.

Despite all this expert help, the Nile proved more difficult than

The Balkan crisis, 1878
As a result of a war between Russia and Turkey, Russian troops were advancing on Constantinople. The Mediterranean fleet was sent up the Dardanelles and the Russians halted their advance

The Lighthouse Battery after the bombardment

The Egyptian war 1882

A mutiny in the Egyptian army threatened British and French control. A British fleet was assembled off Alexandria and, when the mutineers refused to surrender, the forts defending the city were bombarded and silenced

HMS Sultan (1870), Superb (1875) and Inflexible (1876) in action
In all, eight ironclads were present at the battle. Here, three of them attack one of the main forts, the so-called Lighthouse Battery

An Egyptian shell explodes on the upper deck of HMS Alexandra (1875)
The officer is Staff Captain Henry Hosken who was responsible for navigating the flagship through the shallow water off Alexandria

The main battery of HMS Alexandra (1875) during the action
Gunners in the fleet flagship train their massive ten-inch muzzle-loading gun on its target. Note the 'mantlet' or metal splinter-netting between the guns

HMS Alexandra (1875) after the bombardment
This photograph, taken in Malta after the bombardment shows the
damage caused by shellfire

anyone had imagined. The first boats began their voyage in late
September, 1884 and it was only on December 15 that the army's
headquarters reached Korti, some 250 miles from Khartoum. The
route therefrom lay across the desert (thus avoiding a 400-mile,
rapid-filled bend of the Nile), where the first main battle of the
campaign was fought at Abu Klea, the naval brigade bearing the
brunt of the fighting. On January 20 the advance guard of the relief
force reached the Nile again at Metemeh and there found four
steamers sent by Gordon to meet them. But time was running out
for him. Attempts to push up-river using the steamers failed. One
sortie was made by the steamer *Safieh* under the personal
command of Lord Charles Beresford on Feburary 3-4, 1885.
Although she could manage only two and a half knots against the
powerful Nile current, the steamer reached Wad Habeshi, barely
50 miles from Khartoum. Here she had to run the gauntlet of
enemy forts and the Mahdi's men put a shot through her boiler.
Beresford used the last remaining power to distance the fort and let
go his anchor. After the damaged boilerhead cooled, Chief
Engineer Henry Benbow spent 10 hours shaping a new plate and
bolting it into position under constant fire throughout. Beresford
recommended Benbow for a DSO and later bitterly regretted not
having asked for a VC for him. Certainly he had deserved it.

Eventually, the *Safieh* got under way again. First she went up
river, then turned and, with the full force of the Nile current
behind her, shot past the surprised fort with all guns blazing and
escaped to the north. Such panache was typical of Beresford and,
indeed, of the whole tradition of naval river work. Sadly, however,

The Egyptian challenge
Arabi Pasha (left) the leader of the mutineers defies Vice-Admiral Seymour (right),
the C-in-C of the Mediterranean fleet and, pictured below, the cabin of Commander
Henry Kane of HMS Alexandra (1875) after the bombardment

it had little effect on the outcome of the campaign, for Khartoum had fallen on January 26 and Gordon was dead. According to a number of eye-witnesses, it did however have a strong effect on the Mahdi who felt that the British were invincible on or near water! When the relief force began to retreat once the news of Gordon's death was known, they were not pursued vigorously. Seapower's deterrent effect had reached as far inland as Khartoum.

Beresford's sailors had acted as soldiers for most of the campaign and only took to their native element in its closing stages. The tradition of naval brigades, where sailors actually fought alongside their red- or khaki-coated colleagues had been growing during the early victorian period and reached its peak between 1870 and 1900. Sailors fought in the Ashantee war of 1873, the Zulu war of 1879, the Egyptian campaign of 1882, the Sudan campaigns of 1884-5, 1888 and 1889, the Boer wars of 1880 and 1899-1902, the third China war of 1900 and in the numerous smaller-scale campaigns in the same period. A remarkable record.

Sometimes the sailors and Royal Marines were used simply as foot soldiers. For example, during the 1884-5 Sudan campaign, the Mahdi's victorious forces reached the Red Sea coast where they threatened the British-and-Egyptian held town of Suakin. The defence of the town was organized by the C-in-C East Indies, Rear Admiral Sir William Hewett who, in fact, was given overall command of all the forces in the area — including Egyptian army units. Needless to say he landed a number of seamen and marines who took part in several sorties during one of which a force of some

Shallow drafts were critical
A shallow-draft river gunboat is hauled over shallows of the Shire River in East Africa, and below, HMS Alecto (1882), a sternwheel paddle steamer built specially for service in Africa, in action at Benin, Nigeria, in 1894

148

River warfare

During the numerous colonial wars of the period, sailors were often employed as boatmen on rivers. They transported troops and stores and often became involved in the fighting

3,900 men (including a naval brigade of 115 men and 400 Royal Marine Light Infantry) was surprised at El Teb by a dervish force of more than 10,000. The British force formed a square in the time-honoured fashion and repeatedly repulsed the enemy with machine-gun and rapid rifle fire. Suddenly, a corner of the square gave way and the dervishes began rushing through the gap. Into the breach stepped Captain Arthur Wilson who happened to have marched out with the square that morning, purely as an observer. He laid about him with his sword until its blade broke, and then continued to belabour the tribesmen with fists and sword remains, receiving a scalp wound in the process. His furious attack saved the day and the gap was closed. Wilson, thinking nothing of his escapade, wrote home from his ship, '. . . I have just got back from a very pretty little fight . . .' . He was recommended for the VC — probably to his annoyance, for he was an extremely modest man. When the award was announced, he blamed it on the fact that his scalp wound had bled profusely, appearing more spectacular than in fact it was. '. . . If I could only have got a basin of water and washed my face, I should have escaped notoriety, . . .' he wrote to a friend. Presented with the cross on Southsea Common on June 6, 1885, his laconic diary entry that day is typical, 'Docked ship', he wrote 'Received the VC'.

Sailors were often used because of their particular skills. In Egypt, in 1882, they even ran a train. After the bombardment of Alexandria (see page 135 *et seq*), Arabi's forces retreated inland. The British sent out regular reconnoitring parties which were fired on and casualties were sustained. To the south of Alexandria, the

En route to Khartoum
The gunboat Safieh, commanded by Lord Charles Beresford, in action with forts at Wad Habeshi in February 1885, and pictured below, hauling gunboats up the second cataract of the River Nile during the first Sudan Campaign 1884-5

Sailors ashore

Sailors and Royal Marines were also employed ashore as expert gunners or even as footsoldiers in the famous naval brigades. They turned their hands to so many varied tasks that the victorians nicknamed them 'The Handymen'!

Sailors from HMS Shah take part in the battle of Ginginhlovo during the Zulu War, 1874

terrain was criss-crossed with railway lines; Captains Wilson and Fisher hit on the idea of armouring a train to transport a skirmishing party close to the enemy lines. Formally 'commissioned' on July 26 (the navy has never been able to envisage its men serving in anything that has not been properly commissioned) the train remained in service for nearly two months. To begin with, it was comparatively simple: an engine with its boilers protected by sandbags, coupled to two wagons armed with light machine guns carrying the men who were protected by thin armourplate taken from ship's stores. By the end of its career it was far more elaborate, often consisting of six or eight well-protected trucks. Some 'models' even carried 40-pounder guns on full naval gun carriages. An early use of armoured vehicles in modern land warfare it was to be copied in subsequent campaigns, notably during the second Boer war when Winston Churchill was captured while out on patrol in one. When Wilson was asked whether he or Fisher had been responsible for the idea, he replied with typical modesty '. . . I am sure I cannot tell you as almost every step has been the result of consultation between us . . .'

However sailors were most in demand as artillerymen, partly because long-range artillery and well-trained gun crews were usually in short supply in the areas where the various colonial wars erupted and partly because bluejackets proved extremely good at this particular task — so good, that they captured the public imagination. Fascinated by their sailors manhandling guns over difficult territory, the victorians nicknamed them The Handymen

The African campaigns

There were numerous small-scale campaigns all over Africa during the period 1870-1900. Sailors were frequently employed, and are show left, landing in Gambia, 1894

Sailors clearing the streets of Coomassie during the Ashantee War, 1873

The Armoured train, August 1882
Designed by Captains Fisher and Wilson, this train was used for armed
reconnaissance outside Alexandria.

and demanded re-enactments back in Britain. The first such field
gun drill took place at the Naval Exhibition of 1891 and was the
forerunner of the famous Royal Tournament gun run.

A dramatic demonstration of this skill came in 1899, at the
outbreak of the second Boer war. Within weeks, the fast-moving,
skilful Boers invaded British-held Natal to threaten the key town of
Ladysmith. They had some excellent Creusot and Krupp field
guns with ranges up to 6,500 metres (the famous Long Toms)
while the standard 12-pounder British horse artillery gun could
reach little over 5,000 metres. From the hills surrounding
Ladysmith the Boers began a long-range bombardment which the
British were powerless to prevent. The town would surely fall
within a few days.

However, at Durban was the armoured cruiser HMS *Terrible*,
diverted there while on her way to the China station. Her captain
was Percy Scott, the notable gunnery expert who was later to be a
leading figure in the gunnery revolution of the 1900s. Scott devised
a stationary land carriage for two naval four point seven-inch guns
and these, together with a number of 12-pounders and their crews
under the command of Captain Hedworth Lambton, were put in a
train and rushed to Ladysmith. Arriving only hours before the
Boers closed their ring round the town, they saved the day. The
extreme range of the four point sevens was 9,000 metres: more
than a match for the Boers' Long Toms. There was one moment of
light relief during the ensuing 119-days' siege when, on Christmas
day, the Boers fired into the town a 75 mm Long Tom shell which
had 'A Merry Xmas' painted on it and was found to contain a

152

Egypt and the Sudan
The British were involved in a series of campaigns to maintain their control of Egypt and its troublesome province, the Sudan

The Battle of El Teb February 29, 1884
A typical action of the victorian period. The British are formed in a square. Admiral Hewett is sitting on his horse, to the left. This was drawn on the spot by the *Illustrated London News* artist, Melton Prior

Bluejackets to the fore! Sudan 1885
Sailors haul up their light field gun in true dashing navy style

Christmas pudding. Otherwise the siege was a grim long drawn out affair and Captain Lambton was forced to use his limited ammunition very sparingly.

Captain Scott also devised a mobile carriage for the naval six-inch guns and so a number were used in Lord Robert's drive to the Boer capital of Pretoria in the Transvaal and in General Buller's operations to relieve Ladysmith and clear the Boers from Natal. Naval personnel, under Scott, also undertook the defence of Durban. The sailors enjoyed this relief from their usual routine and were noted for their high spirits. All their guns had nicknames: such as 'Bloody Mary' or 'Little Bobs' (after Lord Roberts whose nickname it was). Indeed, strangely, the army commanders seemed content to use sailors as the spearhead of their assaults even when there were plenty of trained regular soldiers available. This policy led to tragedy. On November 25, a naval brigade under Captain Reginald Prothero was at the head of a column which attacked the Boers at Graspan, close to Bloemfontein. The battle opened with a long-range shelling of the Boer positions after which the brigade deployed into a single line with intervals of four paces. Close order indeed — much closer than the army units were using. They came under a withering fire but continued to advance in rushes, taking cover wherever they could. To set an example to his men, Captain Prothero remained upright and, of course, was severely wounded. The official account says that he was carried 'unwillingly' to the rear which, bearing in mind Prothero's reputation, is probably a masterpiece of understatement. One of his midshipmen, later to become Admiral of the Fleet Lord

154

Welcome home!
Men from HMS Terrible march in triumph through the streets of Portsmouth to a special banquet in the town hall

The Royal Military Tournament, 1900
Sailors from HMS Terrible re-enact their exploits. This demonstration led to the regular field gun runs which are such a popular feature of the Royal Tournament today, below, a naval four-point-seven inch gun on the way to the relief of Ladysmith, February 1900

The Boer War

The largest-scale of all the colonial wars. It lasted for three years and involved many thousands of men. Sailors and Royal Marines from the armoured cruisers, HMS Powerful and Terrible, particularly distinguished themselves with their mobile, long-range guns

Cunningham, described him thus, '. . . He was a most intimidating man, nearly six feet tall and immensely broad with a heavy, jet-black beard . . . he was known as Prothero the Bad . . .'. The attack went on and still the men fell, including a midshipman, Cymbeline Huddart who, though twice wounded, continued to press on until he was mortally hit. He received posthumously the newly created Conspicuous Service Cross (forerunner of the DSC) and Prothero was so affected by his courage that he presented his own sword to the boy's parents in his memory. Finally, however, the decimated brigade managed to struggle to the top of the hill from which the Boers had been firing. Their extraordinary gallantry had won the day — but at a cost. Out of 195 officers and men engaged 15 were killed and 70 wounded.

Losses such as these — due partly to insufficient training and lack of experience — highlighted the fact that sailors were being misused. As gunners, the sailors obviously had an important role to play, but as soldiers they were now far less necessary. As the empire had grown, so too had the regular forces in the various colonies. In fact, the Boer war and the third China war — which occurred at almost exactly the same time — were the last major colonial wars to involve sailors. In 1904, Fisher the great reformer became First Sea Lord and the police force image was ruthlessly swept away.

To understand Fisher's reforms, it is necessary to turn briefly once more to the international scene. Throughout the 19th century, Britain's naval supremacy had been based on the fact that no other country had a fleet large enough to challenge the Royal

155

HMS Fame (1896) bombarding the Taku forts, June 17 1900
The Fame and her near-sister HMS Whiting (1896) both played an active role in this
battle. They were thus the first British destroyers to go into action

The third China War

In 1900, Britain and other major powers became involved in a war in China over the Boxer rebellion. British sailors and Royal Marines served ashore and ships of the East Indies fleet bombarded key positions

Navy, even two combined navies, such as France and Russia who were considered the most likely enemies, were insufficient to alter the balance. This Two-Power Standard concept was first expressed in 1889 by the First Sea Lord, but in practice it had existed for some years.

In the late 1890s, however, the balance began to shift. Germany, under the twin influences of Kaiser Wilhelm II and Admiral von Tirpitz, began building, almost from scratch, a sizeable fleet. Two navy laws were passed, in 1898 and 1900 by which Germany was to have a fleet of 34 battleships by 1917, enabling her to take the place among the world powers, hitherto, denied her. The preamble to the 1900 law stated, '. . . Germany must have a battlefleet so strong that, even for the strongest sea power, war against it would invite such dangers as to imperil its position in the world . . .'

In Britain, there was no doubt as to who the preamble's 'strongest sea power' was. From the first, these navy laws were seen as a deliberate threat to British naval supremacy, made worse by Germany's growing industrial and economic strength which now rivalled Britain's and enabled her to build a new fleet expeditiously. The British view, although somewhat exaggerated, was close to the truth. Tirpitz' aim clearly was to create a navy so strong that Britain could not hope to fight it without serious losses. In the face of such a threat, he confidently expected that Britain would grant major concessions in matters of colonial and foreign policy, thus giving Germany her coveted 'place in the sun', to use a phrase of the Kaiser's.

Both Tirpitz and the Kaiser seem naively to have assumed that

Unveiling the China Memorial in Victoria Park, Portsmouth
Standing left are Admiral Sir Edward Seymour (C-in-C East Indies during the war) and Captain John Jellicoe (of World War One fame) who was Captain of Seymour's flagship, HMS Centurion (1892)

Britain would allow such a fleet without countering it. Certainly, some sections of the British press seemed prepared to accept the Germans' protestations that the new fleet was defensive. But, when the naval law of 1898 was followed by that of 1900 and by a further extension in 1902, and when the Germans were seen to adopt such an anti-British attitude during the Boer war, then public opinion began to swing violently against Germans. British foreign policy underwent a major change. Within the space of four years, Britain had made a formal naval alliance with Japan; an informal agreement — known as *L'Entente Cordiale* — with the French; and another naval agreement with the United States. Alliances had been discussed, even negotiated, in the 1890s but never with such urgency.

At the Admiralty too, attitudes changed, especially when the first German battleships built under the 1898 law, the *Wittlesbach* class, appeared. They were clearly designed for the North Sea only with a cruising radius of only 4,000 miles at 10 knots compared with the 7,200 miles at 10 knots of their British contemporaries, the *Duncan* Class; while their cramped crew quarters were designed to be occupied only for short periods. Almost overnight Germany replaced France and Russia as the most likely opponent in a future war. In 1903 it was announced that a new naval base would be established at Rosyth on the Firth of Forth, opposite Germany's main naval base at Kiel. In 1904, the old Home fleet was reorganised; obsolescent reserve ships gave way to six *Royal Sovereigns* and two brand-new *Duncans*. At the same time, the Channel fleet was increased from six to eight

Naval manoeuvres

In 1887 manoeuvres were held following the great fleet review held to celebrate Queen Victoria's golden jubilee. They were so successful that they were repeated annually and many lessons were learned that were to prove useful in wartime

first class battleships.

So, when Fisher arrived at Admiralty on Trafalgar Day, 1904 an important shift had already been made in British naval policy. With typical drive and enthusiasm, he turned the shift into a reversal; scrapping many ageing vessels of all sizes still retained either in reserve or in the many worldwide squadrons. His more swingeing cuts were prevented by Lord Selbourne, the First Lord, but nonetheless 154 vessels, mostly small cruisers, went for scrap, enabling Fisher to carry out his pet 'nucleus crew' scheme. It also necessitated a drastic reorganisation of the Navy's deployment resulting in a veritable 'recall of the legions'. The independent Pacific and South American commands vanished, together with the bases in the West Indies and at Esquimault. The East Indies, China and Australian squadrons were merged into one Far East fleet based on Singapore. The Mediterranean fleet, once the pride and showpiece of the Royal Navy, was steadily reduced from 15 of the latest battleships in 1903, to six, all of them pre-dreadnoughts, by 1910. At the same time, Fisher master-minded a major build-up in home waters. The old Channel fleet disappeared altogether to be replaced, by 1910, with a Home fleet of two active divisions each of eight battleships, supported by five armoured or battle cruisers and 25 destroyers. In addition there was an Atlantic fleet of six battleships and four armoured cruisers based on Gibraltar. In time of emergency, a force of 23 battleships (eight of them dreadnoughts) and 13 armoured or battle cruisers could be concentrated immediately. And, within a few days, thanks to the 'nucleus crew' system, another 23 reserve battleships could be put

The wardroom of HMS Northumberland (1866)
Newspaper artists and correspondents were allowed aboard the ships to report on the manoeuvres. The artist here seems to have been particularly struck by the Northumberland's rolling!

The attack on Liverpool, 1888
Ships of Sir George Tryon's squadron bombard the forts at the mouth of the Mersey prior to demanding the surrender of Liverpool

into active service with large numbers of cruisers and destroyers. It was remarkable reorganisation, of immense complexity, carried through in the teeth of considerable opposition by the unique drive and determination of Fisher — aided and protected by successive First Lords and by King Edward VII whose help, Fisher acknowledged, was decisive.

At the same time there was an equally dramatic change in fleet activity. Hitherto, the main squadrons had cruised leisurely from port to port with occasional exercises in 'steam tactics', in which the ships practised complicated dance-like manoeuvres with infrequent gun practices. As we have seen, a major revolution in gun practice began around 1900 and this was matched by a more realistic approach to war and battle practice.

In 1887, following the great review held at Spithead to celebrate the Diamond Jubilee of Queen Victoria, it was decided that before the ships dispersed they should manoeuvre as two supposedly hostile forces. So many lessons were learned from these new-style exercises that they were continued annually. In 1888 the aim was to discover whether the Napoleonic war strategy of close blockade of enemy harbours was still practical in an age of torpedo boats, mines and steam-propelled warships. The blockaded admiral, Sir George Tryon, proved most dramatically that it was not, by slipping with his entire fleet past his 'enemy', sending his cruisers to 'bombard' Aberdeen, Edinburgh, Newcastle, Grimsby and Hull while he took his heavy ships up the Mersey to Liverpool. After a thunderous barrage of blanks, he sent a message to the Lord Mayor stating that, in return for a cessation of hostilities, 'his

161

Worship and his successors should be compelled, if asked, to dine
with the Admiral and his succesors at least once a year'.

Subsequent manoeuvres were as conclusive. Torpedo boats
were tested with the fleet at sea in 1889 and failed to live up to
expectations; convoys were tried in 1890; the scouting abilities of
cruisers in 1897; submarines in 1903; wireless in 1906. Thus a fund
of experience began to build up that was to prove invaluable
during the 1914-18 war. For example, in 1901, the C-in-C of the
Channel fleet, Sir Arthur Wilson, as an experiment, approached
his 'enemy' with his ships in columns and then deployed into line
ahead at the last moment, instead of forming his line in the early
stages as had been the usual practice before. On May 31, 1916
Admiral Sir John Jellicoe used this precise tactic at the beginning of
the Battle of Jutland.

The new realism was not confined simply to the annual
manoeuvres. Fleet admirals were also revolutionising the day-to-
day activities of their ships. In the Mediterranean, between 1891
and 1893, the victor of the 1889 manoeuvres, Sir George Tryon,
delighted in devising complicated exercises designed to test the
abilities of his captains to the limit. His rule was never to explain or
to discuss his full intentions until the evolution had been com-
pleted, so that the conditions would be as realistic as possible. In
June 1893, this led to a tragedy which cost him his life. The fleet
was steaming into the anchorage at Tripoli in two columns, one
headed by Tryon in his flagship HMS *Victoria* and the other by the
second in command — Albert Markham of Arctic fame — in HMS
Camperdown. Tryon signalled that the columns, then 1,200 yards

**Close water-tight doors!
Annual manoeuvres 1895**

The battle of Belfast, 1894
The opposing fleets clash off
Belfast. Note how close-
range the action is. The great
gunnery revolution is still a
few years away

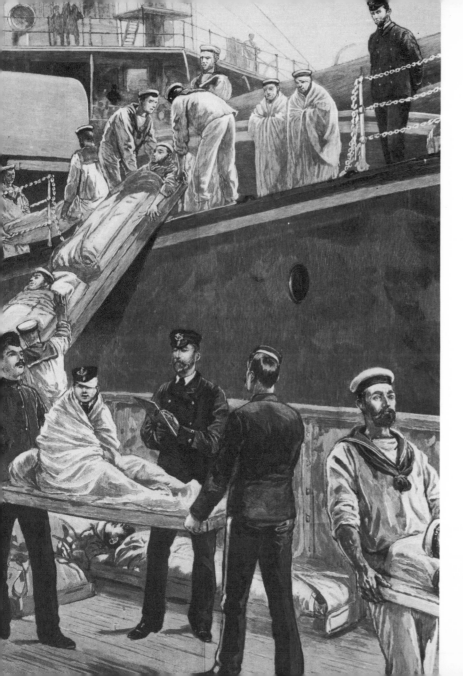

apart, should turn inwards so that the ships would be in their correct positions for anchoring. This was very dangerous, since the minimum turning circle of the ships was 800 yards which meant that, for safety, the columns should have been more than 1,600 yards apart. The problem was that no-one except Tryon knew what was intended. Did he really want the ships to turn in together, so that they ended up in two lines close to each other? If he did, then he made a fatal mistake in not ensuring that the columns were further apart to begin with. Or did he have something more spectacular in mind? Certainly, as the signal fluttered at the *Victoria*'s yardarm, that is what some of Tryon's subordinates thought.

'Now we shall see something interesting. How on earth are we going to do it?' said Captain Arthur Moore of HMS *Dreadnought*. In HMS *Camperdown*, however, there was consternation. For a few minutes Admiral Markham and his staff discussed the seemingly impossible order and delayed acknowledging the C-in-C's signal. Then the semaphore on the bridge of the *Victoria* was seen to be working.

'What are you waiting for?' came the angry signal. At that moment, Markham suddenly guessed — or thought he guessed — Tryon's intention: the ships of the *Victoria*'s column would not turn as sharply as those of the *Camperdown*'s division and so would circle outside of them, passing port side to port side as the Rule of the Road at Sea dictated. Accordingly, he acknowledged Tryon's signal, which was then hauled down and the manoeuvre began but, to the horror of all who were watching, the *Victoria* turned

Landing the 'wounded' 1892
Note the midshipman who doesn't seem to appreciate the seriousness of his wound!

with exactly the same amount of helm, so that a collision was unavoidable and the *Camperdown*'s sharp ram tore into the starboard bow of the *Victoria* making a huge hole. Such a blow was serious but should not have been fatal. Tryon at once ordered the *Camperdown* to back off and headed his flagship for the shore, hoping to beach her and effect repairs. The *Victoria* had hardly got under way again however, before her entire foredeck was awash and her list increased with frightening speed. Finally, less than eight minutes after the *Camperdown* had struck, she lurched into starboard and sank with 258 officers and men — including Tryon who was heard to mutter, 'It was all my fault'.

The significance of this famous incident has been much exaggerated in the past. Tryon had a reputation as a fierce and overbearing commander, whose subordinates were afraid of questioning his orders and this blind obedience has been cited as a typical example of the archaic way in which the late victorian navy worked. In fact, in the moments before the manoeuvre, Tryon's own officers repeatedly questioned him about the short distance between the columns and were repeatedly rebuffed. Either this was incredible stubbornness or he did really have 'something up his sleeve'. It has been suggested, for example, that he wanted Markham's column to circle round *him* — in other words the exact opposite of what Markham thought he intended. The truth will never be known. In any case, Tryon's well-known temper was not typical. Fisher, Beresford, Wilson, Prince Louis of Battenburg and numerous other fleet commanders of the time were just as innovative as Tryon but they combined this gift with an ability to communicate their wishes and the thinking behind them to their subordinates.

Moreover, the *Victoria-Camperdown* collision was not an isolated incident, though its tragic and dramatic proportions have made it particularly notorious. There were numerous other accidents in the period 1890 to 1910. In 1892, the battleship HMS *Howe* grounded in Ferrol Harbour during manoeuvres with the Channel fleet. In 1903, the battleship *Prince George* was rammed by HMS *Hannibal* off Cape Finisterre while the Channel fleet was practising night steaming without navigation lights. In 1906, the battleship HMS *Montagu* went aground off Lundy Island while the Channel fleet was engaged in exercises in thick fog. And, in 1908, there was an almost exact reproduction of the *Victoria-Camperdown* incident in which disaster was averted by the presence of mind and initiative of Rear Admiral Sir Percy Scott, in command of the 1st Cruiser squadron attached to the Channel fleet under Lord Charles Beresford. Beresford ordered Scott's cruisers, which were in two divisions, to execute an inward turn, when the distance between them was only 1,200 yards. Scott saw the danger, refused to acknowledge the signal and turned his ship in the opposite direction. Although Beresford later approved Scott's action, this incident occurred at the height of the Fisher-Beresford feud noted earlier and so, since Scott was recognised as a protegé of Fisher's, the incident was seized on by the press as another attack by Fisher's party on Beresford's authority.

Such accidents and near misses did not mean that the Royal Navy was becoming more inefficient. Rather, they were an

BROADSIDE

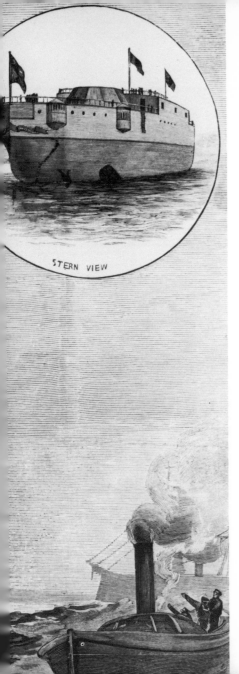

STERN VIEW

The launch of HMS Camperdown at Portsmouth, November 24, 1885
Her powerful ram which so badly damaged HMS Victoria can be seen clearly

The Victoria disaster

One of the early exponents of realistic war practice was Sir George Tryon. He delighted in devising complicated evolutions which stretched the skill of his office to the limit. On June 22, 1893 he was drowned when his flagship HMS Victoria (1887) was rammed and sunk by HMS Camperdown (1885) when one of the evolutions went badly wrong

indication of the greatly increased realism — and consequently the increased risks — of late victorian and edwardian battle-training. Most of the sea-going admirals during the period 1890-1910 contributed to this realism but probably its greatest exponent was Sir Arthur Wilson.

Wilson has appeared frequently in these pages: as a torpedo pioneer and expert; as an inventor; as a modest winner of a VC. But undoubtedly his greatest contribution to the service he loved was the way in which he prepared it for war during his unique six-year command in the Channel between 1901 and 1907. No other peace-time admiral held a command for so long and he was able to stamp his own remarkable personality on the fleet. He was a superb seaman, renowned for his physical and moral toughness — the seamen called him 'Old 'Ard 'Eart' — who ruthlessly drove the ships and men under his command. He even took the ships to sea during the cherished Christmas leave period and, on one occasion was supposed to have personally navigated his fleet of 12 battleships into Arosa Bay in thick fog, by having the sea gangway of his flagship lowered so that he could look under the fog, less dense close to the water. Fisher's brilliance — like Nelson's — has tended to overshadow his equally gifted contemporaries and Wilson has suffered undeserved obscurity since the first world war. But the esteem in which he was held can be judged by the fact that he and Fisher were the only admirals of that period who received the coveted Order of Merit with Swords. Fisher's award was dated 1905; Wilson received his in 1911. Administratively, the Grand fleet of 1914-18 may be fairly said to be Fisher's creation: in practical and morale terms, it was Wilson's.

This growing realism was much applauded at the time, although some of Fisher's reforms — particularly his belligerent achieving of them — aroused naval opposition. It has also been approvingly endorsed by successive generations of historians. As a world war loomed on the horizon, any measures that made the Royal Navy more ready for that war were clearly desirable and right.

There are two possible objections to this approach. First, it is based on hindsight. To us the first world war now seems to have been inevitable. But was it at the time? Certainly there seems to have been what almost amounts to a *desire* for war in the early 1900s: a feeling that Europe in general and Britain in particular were decadent and that a war would have a cleansing and strengthening effect. Ernle Chatfield, Admiral Beatty's flag captain at Jutland recorded in his memoirs that Beatty 'longed' for war. 'We had not fought for a century: it was time we repeated the deeds of our forefathers'. And the novelist Conan Doyle, writing in 1914, put these words into the mouth of his famous detective hero, Sherlock Holmes.

'There is an east wind coming Watson . . . such a wind as never blew on England yet. It will be cold and bitter, Watson, and a good many of us may wither before its blast. But it's God's own wind nonetheless, and a cleaner, better, stronger land will lie in the sunshine when the storm has cleared.'

In such an atmosphere, it is at least arguable that Britain's new naval policies of the edwardian period made war even more likely.

168

After the collision
HMS Victoria begins to settle in the water. To the left, can be seen HMS Camperdown which has gone astern to get clear

The concentration of the fleets in home waters was an unmistakable signal to the Germans that they were regarded as the major foe and that Britain was prepared to abandon her worldwide interests in order the crush Germany. At the same time, the building of the *Dreadnought*, while justified in purely naval terms, was a deliberate abandonment of the British supremacy of numbers which had so effectively deterred her rivals in the past, since Britain was unable to build ships sufficiently fast to gain her old supremacy. In 1914, Britain had only 25 dreadnoughts and nine battle-cruisers, compared with Germany's 13 dreadnoughts and three battle-cruisers — a far narrower margin than at the outset of any other war in her history. Above all, the launching of the *Dreadnought* and the constant narrowness of the margin led to an hysterical numbers game when Britain seemed to be falling behind. 'We want eight and we won't wait' was the popular cry in 1908. Such hysteria must be seen as an important contributory factor to the outbreak of war.

Secondly, by no means all of the innovations helped Britain in war time. The obsession with new types of ship — dreadnoughts and submarines — ensured that Britain entered the war with an unbalanced fleet. The ruthless scrapping policy of the early 1900s meant that there were only 74 small cruisers in service in 1914 and this lack of ships to defend the trade routes was to be felt acutely when the war came — especially after the Germans introduced unrestricted U-boat warfare and convoys became necessary. By 1918 more than 200 cruisers, sloops and patrol boats had been added to the fleet to fill this gap. Moreover, the powerful and 169

Vice-Admiral Sir George Tryon KCB

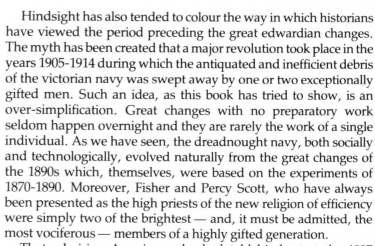

Hindsight has also tended to colour the way in which historians have viewed the period preceding the great edwardian changes. The myth has been created that a major revolution took place in the years 1905-1914 during which the antiquated and inefficient debris of the victorian navy was swept away by one or two exceptionally gifted men. Such an idea, as this book has tried to show, is an over-simplification. Great changes with no preparatory work seldom happen overnight and they are rarely the work of a single individual. As we have seen, the dreadnought navy, both socially and technologically, evolved naturally from the great changes of the 1890s which, themselves, were based on the experiments of 1870-1890. Moreover, Fisher and Percy Scott, who have always been presented as the high priests of the new religion of efficiency were simply two of the brightest — and, it must be admitted, the most vociferous — members of a highly gifted generation.

That admiring American who had told his host at the 1897 Jubilee Review, 'I guess sir, this makes for peace', was right at the time he spoke. The deterrent effect of the Royal Navy in 1897 and its firm grip on world wide affairs was still considerable while its day-to-day duties could nearly all be categorised as 'peace-keeping'. By 1910, that judgment would have been wrong. Highly concentrated, over specialised, concerned above all with power, speed and efficiency, the Royal Navy was actively preparing for what Fisher revealingly — and, to modern eyes, frighteningly — called Armageddon, the supreme and final conflict of the nations. It had ceased to be a force for peace and had become, for the first time in its history, a potential catalyst for war.

vastly expensive battleships proved to be white elephants. Neither side was prepared to risk their fleets and, as a result, the surface naval war, like the land war, was largely a stalemate with few decisive actions. At sea, the really decisive campaign was in fact the U-boat war on trade — a campaign which Germany nearly won because of Britain's lack of preparation. So, the traditional view of the Fisher era is open to some reinterpretation.

The last lurch
HMS Victoria begins to sink as her crew abandon ship. Her propellors are still turning

The Victoria court-martial on board HMS Hibernia (1805) in Malta Grand Harbour
Rear-Admiral Sir Albert Markham, Tryon's second in command
(standing left), is giving evidence

The last of HMS Victoria
A dramatic photograph, taken with a primitive box camera by Staff Surgeon James
Collot who was in HMS Collingwood 1882

The fleet that Wilson trained
The combined Channel and Home Fleets exercising together in 1906

Admiral of the Fleet Sir Arthur Wilson VC

The greatest sea-going admiral of the edwardian period. During his unusually long spell in command of the forces in the Channel (1901-7) he prepared the fleet for war with rigorous training and realistic battle practice. He was known by the sailors as Old 'Ard 'Eart, shown on the right shortly after his promotion to flag rank in 1895

Abu Klea, battle of 2-147
Achilles 1-36, -39, 46 / **2-97**
Acre, bombardment of 1-57, -134
Active **2-60**, **-74**
Admiralty 1-14, -16, -42, -45, -46, **-49**, -59, **-64**, -67 / 2-9, -10, -12, -26, -49, -52, -87, **-88**, -99, -103, -105, -158
Adventure **2-57**, -141
Africa 2-65
Agamemnon (1852) **1-25**, -29, -129, **-135**
Agamemnon (1879) 2-20
Agincourt **1-35**, 1-46, -49 / 2-69
Ajax (1809) 1-27
Ajax (1880) 2-20
Alberta 1-99 / **2-110**, **-112**, **-113**, -114
Albert, Prince Regent 1-94, -96, -99 -100, **-105**, **-106**, -108, **-110**, -113 / 2-9, -114, -118
Albert, Prince (George VI) 2-110
Albert Edward, Prince of Wales (King Edward VII) **1-80**, **-94**, -106, **-114**, **-116** / **2-12**, **-47**, 70, -85, **-99**, -102, -104, -106, -107, **-109**, -113, -114, **-119**, -121, **-125**, -161
Albion 1-64, **-157**
Alecto (1839) 1-19, **-21**, -27
Alecto (1882) **2-148**
Alexandra 2-14, **-25**, -30, -49, -67, -100, -109, **-123**, **-145**, **-147**
Alexandra, Princess, of Wales (Queen) 1-117 / **2-12**, -14, -85, -102, **-107**, **-110**, **-123**, **-125**, -128
Alexandria, bombardment of 2-14, -20, -49, -102, -103, -135, **-144**, **-145**, -149, -152
Alfred, Duke of Edinburgh **1-94**, **-95**, **-96**, -106, -108 / 2-14, -70, -99 et seq, **-99**, **-100**, -107, -109
Amethyst 2-51, **-57**
Amphion **1-23**, -27
Amundsen, Capt Roald 2-131, -138
Arab **1-126**
Arabi Pasha, Col 2-103, -134, -135, **-147**
Ariadne **2-61**, -102
Armour plating 1-40, -42, -45, 46 / 2-8, **-12**, -33, -53, -54
Armoured batteries 1-30, -40
Armoured trains 2-149 et seq, **2-152-3**
Arthur, Capt Wm 2-59, -60, -62

Asia 1-15
Audacious 2-12, -52
Aviation, naval 2-65, **-66**, **-67**
Azoff, Sea of 1-145

Bacchante 2-107
Balkan Crisis, The (1878) 2-99, -134, **-142**
Ballard, Admiral George 1-78
Baltic Fleet **1-118**, **-119**
Barbettes 2-14, -22, -26, **-33**, -39
Barnaby, Sir Nathaniel 2-26
Beagle, 1-131, **-136**, -138, **-139**
Beaufort, Sir Francis 1-131 / 2-131
Bechervaise, John 1-74, -77, -79
Bellerophon (1865) 2-8, -12, **-21**
Bellerophon (1907) **2-45**
Benbow **2-34**
Benbow, Chief Engineer Henry 2-147
Beresford, Admiral Lord Charles 2-30, -36, -39, -79, **-81**, **-82**, -84, -110, -142, -147, **-149**, -159, -165
Birkenhead **1-127-8**, -34
Black Prince **1-35**, -46, -106 / 2-99
Blake 2-51
Boadicea 2-52
Bomarsund, bombardment of 1-143
Brassey, Thomas, MP 2-70
Brisk 1-127
Bristol 2-8
Britannia (1820) 1-67, **-79** / **2-77**, -107
Britannia (1953) 2-113
Britannia Royal Naval College, Dartmouth **2-76**, -78
Brooke, 'Rajah' James 1-125, -126
Brown, Capt J H 1-69 / 2-69
Bulldog **1-153**
Burgin, Joseph **1-87**
Burgoyne, Capt Hugh 2-8

Cable laying 1-129, **-135**, **-136**
Caesar **1-61**, **-69**
Caledonia **1-42**, -46
Calliope **2-53**
Calypso 2-74
Cambrian 2-103
Camperdown 2-162, -164, -165, **-167**, -168
Canopus **2-43**

Canton 1-136, -137, **-145**
Capper, Henry 2-87
Captain **2-8**, -12, **-14**, -18, -19
Carmichael, J **1-72**
Carysfort 2-49
Central batteries 2-12, -14, **-20**, **-21**, **-22**, **-23**, **-24**, **-25**, **-145**
Chaplains **1-69**, **-71**, **-72**, **-76**
Charlotte Dundas 1-12
Chatham **1-37**, -46 / **2-34**, -75
Centurion 2-157
Cerberus 2-19
Challenger 2-131, **-135**
Chatfield, Capt Ernle 2-168
Childers, Mid 2-8
Churchill, Sir Winston 2-151
Classes of ships: *Admiral* 2-26, -33, **-34**, 36; *Archer* 2-51; *Cadmus* 2-49; *Canopus* 2-33; *Cressy* 2-53; *Cyclops* 2-19; *Duncan* 2-36, -158; *Edgar* 2-56; *Formidable* 2-33; *King Edward VII* 2-36, -42; *London* 2-33; *Majestic* 2-33; *Minotaur* 2-54, -57; *Orlando* 2-51; *Pallas* 2-56; *Royal Sovereign* 2-33, -43, **-96**, -158; *Wittlesbach* (German) 2-158
Coastguard **2-70**
Cockburn, Admiral Sir George 1-60
Codrington, Admiral Sir Henry 1-45
Coles, Capt Cowper 2-8, -9, -10, -12, -14, -18, -19
Colonial Wars: Abyssinian 1867/8 1-141 **-147**; Ashantee 1873 2-148, **-151**; Benin 1894 **2-148**; Second Boer 1899-1902 2-138 et seq, -151, -152 et seq, **-155**; First Burma 1824-26 1-135, **-144**; Second Burma 1850-53 1-135; Carlist 1837 1-138; First China 1840-42 1-135, -136, **-145**; Second China 1857-60 1-135, -137, **-145**, **-146**; Third China 1900 2-148, -155, **-156**, **-157**; Egyptian 1882 2-100, -103, -134 et seq, **-144** et seq, -148, -149 / **2-152-3**; Gambia 1894 **2-150**; Indian Mutiny 1857 1-139, -147; Japanese 1863-4 1-134, **-139**, **-142**; Second New Zealand 1860-66 1-140, **-147**; Nyassa, Lake 1893-4 2-141, **-148**; First Sudan 1884 2-142, -148, **-149**,

-153; Syrian 1840 1-133, **-139**; Zulu 1879 2-148, -151
Collingwood 1-46 / 2-26, **-36**, -171
Colossus (1848) 1-53
Colossus (1882) 2-20
Colossus (1910) **2-44**
Comet 1-12
Conqueror (1833) **1-25**, -45
Conqueror (1911) **2-50**
Conway 1-70
Cooke, T P **1-81**, **-82** / 2-84
Corbett, Sir Julian 2-84
Crescent 2-51
Crimean War 1854-56 1-39, -67, -69, **-73**, -89, -118, -129, -142, **-148** et seq / 2-29, -58, -69, -70
Cruiser **1-150**
Cunningham, A F Lord 2-155
Curacoa 1-62
Custance, Admiral Sir Reginald 2-39
Cyclops 1-129

Darwin, Charles 1-131, -136
Defence (1861) **1-44**, **-47**, **-117**
Defence (1907) 2-57
De Lome, Dupuy 1-40
Devastation 2-19, **-22**, -26, -33
Devonport *see* Plymouth
Diana **1-144**
Dido 1-127
Discovery **2-136**, **-137**
Dolphin 2-64
Domville, Admiral Sir Compton 2-39, -70
Donegal **2-96**
Doris **2-90**
Dove 2-141
Dreadnought (1875) 2-19, -20, -103, -109, -164
Dreadnought (1906) 2-19, -36, -43, -44, **-47**, **-48**, -49, -54, -169
Duilio 2-20
Duke of Wellington **1-26**, -45, **-60**, **-118**, **-150**
Duncan **2-97**
Dundas, Admiral Richard **1-60**, -143, -154
Dundonald, Lord (Thomas Cochrane) 1-59
Dunkin, Wm 1-73

Edgar 1-48
Edinburgh 2-20, -85
Edinburgh, Duke of *see* Alfred, Duke of Edinburgh
Edward VII *see* Albert Edward, Prince of Wales
Elfin **1-95**, **-97**, **-100**, **-101**, **-102** / 2-113
El Teb, battle of 2-149, **-153**
Endymion **2-56**
Engineering branch 1-14, **-34**, -60, -62, **-73** / **2-78**
Erebus 1-131, **-139**
Ericsson, John 2-9
Escape Creek, battle of **1-55**
Europa 2-67
Euryalus **1-94**, -106, -148
Eurydice 1-12, **2-75**
Excellent 1-27, -68, **-80**, -134, -138 / 2-29, -60, -77, -79, -107
Exmouth 1-154
Exploration 1-131, **-138**, **-139** / 2-131, **-136**, **-137 -138**, **-139**

Fairy 1-97, **-101**, -103, **-113**, **-119**
Falkland Islands, battle of 2-58
Fame **2-156**
Fatshan Creek, battle of 1-137, **-146**
Ferret **2-63**
Fisher, A F Lord 2-29, -36, -39, -43, -44, -46, -51, -59, -60, -62, -65, -72, -75, **-77**, -78, -79, -81, -103, -105, -119, -136, -151, -152, -155, -159, -161, -165, -167, -168, -170
Fitzclarence, Capt Lord Adolphus 1-108
Fitzroy, Capt Robert 1-131, -136, **-138**
Fleet Reviews: 1827 **1-92**; 1845 1-100; 1853 1-103, -118; 1856 1-105, **-120**, **-121**; 1867 1-106; 1873 2-118, **-124**; 1878 2-118, -119, **-125**; 1886 2-118; 1887 **1-35** / 2-29, -30, -118, -119, -161; 1889 2-104, -106, -118; 1891 **2-125**, **-126**; 1897 2-118, -119, -121, **-127**; 1902 2-118, -119, -121; 1905 2-118; 1911 2-118; 1914 2-105
Flying Fish **1-10**
Franklin, Capt Sir John 1-131, **-139** / 2-131
Furious **1-55**

Index

Pages prefixed 1- refer to volume one in the series, *The end of the sailing navy*, 2- refer to the current volume. Page numbers in bold indicate illustration in text

G *alatea* **1-95, -96,** -106 / 2-99
Gambier, Cdr J W 1-140
Ganges 1-15 / 2-77
Garibaldi, Guiseppi **1-132,** -133
Gate Pa, attack on **1**-147
George IV 1-93, -96, -98
George V 1-108 / 2-107 et seq, **2-108, 2-110**
Gilbert, Sir W S 2-84
Ginginhlovo, battle of **2-151**
Gladiator **1-16,** -19, -29
Gladstone, Wm MP **2-113**
Glatton (1855) **1-30**
Glatton (1871) **2-14**
Good Hope **2-56**
Gorgon 1-62
Graspan, battle of 2-154
Greenwich Pensioners **1-87**
Greenwich Royal Hospital School **1-75**
Gunboats: Crimean 1-50, **-51** et seq; River 2-139 et seq, **2-148-9**
Gunnery, development of: Breechloaders v. muzzleloaders 1-46 / 2-20, -22; cordite 2-39; fire control 2-39, -42, **-44;** rifling 1-45, shells 1-33, -34; training 1-68, **-80** / 2-70
Guns, types of: Breechloaders 110pdr **1-32,** 110 ton **2-11;** Gatling 2-63, **-102,** -103; Muzzleloaders 56pdr **1-155,** 6 inch **2-10,** 10 inch **2-145,** 11 inch **2-25,** 16 inch **2-20, -33;** Nordenfeldt 2-63

H all, Capt W H 1-136, -145, **-153**
Hannibal (1854) 1-133, -134
Hannibal (1896) 2-165
Harding, Gunner Israel, VC 2-14
Harris, Capt Robert 1-67
Harvey, Capt John 2-59, -62
Havock 2-63
Hay, Admiral Lord John 2-100
Hecla (1839) 1-136, **-153**
Hecla (bought 1878) **2-60,** -62
Heneage, Admiral Sir Algernon 'Pompo' 2-78
Herald 2-141
Hercules **2-20,** -30
Hero (1858) **1-115**

Hero (1885) 2-82, **-83**
Hewett, Admiral Sir Wm, VC 2-30, -148, **-153**
Hibernia (1805) **2-171**
Hibernia (1905) 2-65, **-67**
HMS Pinafore (Opera) **2-84**
Holland Three (submarine) **2-64**
Holman, Thomas 1-79
Hood (1918) 2-58
Hornby, Admiral Sir Geoffrey Phipps 2-134
Howe 2-165
Huascar **2-53,** -60
Humber 2-136
Hydrography 1-131, **-136,** 2-131, **-135**

I brahim Pasha 1-133-4
Illustrious 1-67-8
Imperieuse 2-52, **-54**
Implacable 2-103, -105
Impregnable 1-94
Inconstant **1-50** / 2-49, -102, -107
Inflexible (1876) 2-20, -22, **-32, -33,** -119, -136, **-144**
Inflexible (1907) 2-58
Invincible (1869) **2-22**
Invincible (1907) 2-54, **-58**
Iphigenia 2-58
Iris 2-49
Iron Duke **2-6, -37,** -52, **-76**
Irresistible **2-94**

J ames Watt 1-29
Jane's Fighting Ships 2-42
Janus 1-94
Jellicoe, A F Earl 1-143 / **2-157,** -162
Jennings, R V 2-72
Juno 2-67
Jutland, battle of 2-110, -162

K agoshima, bombardment of 1-46, 1-135 / 2-20
Kaiser, Wilhelm 2-79, -88, **-104-5,** -106, -118, -157

Kane, Cdr Henry **2-147**
Keppel, Admiral Sir Henry 1-127, -128, -132, -146, **-147**
Key, Admiral Sir Astley Cooper 1-62, -65, **-74**
Khedive Tewfik 2-29, -134, -135
Kinburn, bombardment of **1-29,** -40, -145
King Edward VII **2-42,** -48, 2-79, -93
Kipling, Rudyard 2-84
Kuper, V-Admiral Augustus 1-135

L ady Nancy (raft) 2-9
Ladysmith, siege of 2-152, -154, -155
La Gloire **1-27,** 1-30, -35, -40, -42, -45
Lambton, Capt Hedworth 2-152, -154
Laughton, Sir John 2-84
Leopard **1-17**
Lightning (1823) **1-92**
Lightning (1877) 2-60, -62
Little, Admiral Sir Charles **2-64**
Lively 2-100
London 2-89
Lord Clyde 1-46
Lord Nelson **2-47**
Lord Warden 1-46, **-47**
Louis Phillipe, King **1-105**
Louis, Prince, of Battenburg (Marquis of Milford Haven) 1-108 / 2-99, **-102** et seq, -165
Lyons, Admiral Lord 1-40

M cLintock, Cdr Francis 1-131, -132, **-139** / 2-131
Maeander **1-128,** -132
Magdala 2-19
Mahdi, The 2-142, -148
Majestic 2-38, -85 **-90**
Malta **1-22** / **2-32, -116, -128**
Manoeuvres, annual: General 2-36, **-159,** -161 et seq; 1888 **2-94, -160-1;** 1889 2-162; 1890 **2-6,** -162; 1892 **2-164,** -165; 1894 **2-161;** 1895 **2-91, -163;** 1896 **2-91;** 1897 2-162; 1899 **2-158;** 1903 2-162; 1906 2-162, **-172;** 1907 **2-162-3**
Mariner's Mirror, The 1-78
Markham, Admiral Sir Robert 2-131, -162, -165, **-171**

Marlborough **2-61**
Marryat, Capt Frederick **1-85**
May, Admiral Sir Wm **2-79**
Medals: First China War 1842 1-71, **-88;** CGM 1-73, -89; CSC 2-155; LS & GC 1-70, **-88;** MSM 1-73; Naval Engineers' **1-73;** NGS (1793-1840) 1-71, **-81, -88,** -137; Order of Merit 2-167; Reserve Decoration 2-70; RNR LS & GC 2-70; VC 1-73, **-89, -91** / 2-147, -149, **-173**
Medea 2-70
Medusa 2-70
Mehemet Ali 1-133
Melampus 2-109
Melbourne 1-69
Melville, Lord 1-16
Merchant Shipping Act 1835 1-68
Mercury 2-49
Merlin 1-154
Merrimac **2-16,** -58
Mersey 2-51
Mikasa 2-87
Minotaur 1-46, **-87**
Mistletoe 2-113
Monarch (1868) 2-10, **-18, -37**
Monarch (1911) **2-51**
Monkey 1-12
Monitor 2-9, **-16, -17,** -58
Montagu 2-165
Montagu, Mid Victor 1-137
Moore, Admiral Sir Arthur 2-164
Mosquito 2-141
Mountbatten of Burma, Earl 1-108 / 2-106
Munday, R-Admiral Sir Rodney 1-132, -133

N apier, Admiral Sir Charles 1-59, -103, **-119,** -133, -134, -143, **-149,** -150 / 2-119
Napoleon 1-40
Napoleon III, Emperor 1-40 / 2-130
Nares, Capt George 2-131 -135
National Maritime Museum 2-84
Naval Brigades 1-138, -140, -142, **-145, -147, -158** / 2-147, -148, **-150, -151,** -153, -155
Naval Exhibition 1891 **2-85, -86**

Naval Intelligence Dept 2-87, -103, -105
Naval Rocket Brigade (Abyssinia) **1-147**
Navy and Army Illustrated, The 2-82
Navy Records Society 2-84
Nelson 2-52
Nelson, V-Admiral Lord 1-10, -65, -87, -93 / 2-53, **-86,** -167
Nemesis 1-34, -136, **-145**
Neptune **2-46**
Newbolt, Sir Henry 2-84
Niagara 1-129, **-135, -136**
Nile 2-33
Noel, Admiral Sir Gerard 2-70
Northampton 2-52, -62, -77
Northbrook, Lord 2-29
Northumberland 1-46 / **2-37, -94, -119, -158**

O dessa, bombardment of 1-159, and covers
Odin 1-19
Officers: Conditions **1-60, -61** / **2-89, -90, -96;** Retirement 1-59; Specialisations 1-59, -60; Training 1-65, **-67, -70** / 2-76, **-78;** Uniform **1-61, -64, -66** / 2-80
Ommaney, Admiral Sir John 1-59, **-64**
Orion **2-50**
Orlando 2-52, **-55**
Osborne See V and *A I* (1843)
Osborne II (1870) 1-99 / 2-102, -110, -113, **-119**
Osborne college **2-78,** -106

P akenham, Capt Wm 2-87, -88
Pall Mall Gazette 2-29
Palmerston, Lord 1-133
Parry, Capt Wm 1-131, **-138** / 2-131
Particular Service Squadron 2-29, **-124**
Peel, Capt Wm, VC 1-140, -147
Pegasus 1-93
Pelorus 1-142
Penelope (1829) **1-16,** -19
Penelope (1867) 2-12, -100
Perseus 1-57
Petropavlovsk, attack on 1-59
Philomel **2-56,** -133

175

Phlegethon 1-34, -127
Phoebe **1-62, -66 / 2-79**
Pioneer 2-141
Piracy, operations against **1-124,** -125, -127
Plymouth 1-10, **-134, -135 /** 2-75, -76, -78, -102
Polyphemus 1-125
Portsmouth 1-10, -19, -20, **-33,** -45, **-47,** -67, -68, -79, -80, -92, -97, -103, -104, **-120, -121, -149, -153 /** 2-34, **-47, -64,** -73, -75, -76, -78, **-112,** -135, **-154,** -167
Portsmouth Evening News 2-119, -121
Powerful 2-53, **-55,** -155 and end papers
Price, R-Admiral David 1-59
Prince George 2-165
Prothero, Capt Reginald 2-154

Queen 1-24, -39

Raby, Cdr Henry, VC 1-73
Rainbow 2-72
Rattler **1-19, -21,** -27
Rattlesnake 2-63
Raven 1-81
Rawson, Admiral Sir 'Harry' 2-133, **-141**
Reed, Sir Edward 2-10, -12, **-14,** -18, -21
Reindeer 2-75
Renown (1857) 1-45
Renown(1895) 2-39, -110
Repulse (1868) 1-46
Repulse (1897) 2-116
Resistance **1-47, -117**
Resolution 2-39
Retribution **1-156**
Revenge (1805) 1-10
Revenge (1859) **1-25**
Rodney 1-45
Ross, R-Admiral Sir James 1-131 / 2-131
Rosyth 2-158
Royal Adelaide **1-26**
Royal Albert **1-106**
Royal Alfred 2-102
Royal Arthur **2-121**
Royal Fleet Reserve 2-70
Royal George 1-96, **-98, -102**

Royal Marines 1-67, -73, -77, **-88,** -138 / **-104, -148**
Royal Military Tournament **2-155**
Royal Naval Academy 1-65 / **2-125**
Royal Naval Artillery Volunteers (RNAV) **2-68, -60, -70,** -72
Royal Naval Coast Volunteers 2-70
Royal Naval College Greenwich 2-77, -107
Royal Naval Museum, Portsmouth **1-20, -92, -98, -100, -102 /** 2-75, -84
Royal Naval Reserve (RNR) -68, -69, -70 / 2-69, -70, -72
Royal Naval Volunteer Reserve 2-68, -72
Royal Oak **1-41,** -46, **-50**
Royal Portsmouth Sailors Home 1-77
Royal Sovereign (1804) **1-92**
Royal Sovereign (1857) 2-9, **-12**
Royal Sovereign (1891) 2-33, **-38,** -48, **-120**
Royal visits: Canada 1860 **1-115;** Cornwall 1846 1-97, -112, -113; France 1858 **1-111;** India 1875 **2-118;** Ireland 1849 **1-109, -110;** Portsmouth 1848 1-97, **-101, -105,** 1891 **2-120, -121,** 1906 **2-47;** Malta 1905 **2-116,** 1909 **2-128;** Scotland 1842 1-96, **-102,** 1848 **1-108**
Roxburgh 2-79
Ruby 2-74
Ruddigore (opera) 2-84
Rupert **2-93**

Sailors: Conditions **1-56,** -78, -79 / **2-90, -96, -97;** Continuous Service 1-68; in popular art **1-75, -81, -82, -83, -74, -85 / 2-2, -5, -82, -83, -84, -85;** Training 1-68, **-75, -76, -77, -80 /** 2-72, **-73, -74, -75,** -77; Uniform **1-2, -62, -63, -64,** -78 / **2-75, -90** et seq
St George 2-51, -133
St Jean D'Acre **1-119**
St Vincent 2-73
Safieh 2-147, **-149**
Sail Training Squadron **2-74,** -77
Sans Pareil **2-30,** -33
Satsuma, Daimio of 1-134, **-140**
Scapa Flow 2-105
Scott, Admiral Sir Percy 2-79, **-81,** -82, -85, -152, -154, -165, -170
Scott, Capt Robert 2-131, **-138**

Scourge 2-67
Scout 2-103
Seagull **2-63**
Sebastopol, bombardment of 1-24, -39, -74, -143, **-155, -156**
Selborne, Lord 2-159
Selborne Scheme 2-77, -78
Seppings, Sir Robert 1-11, -14, -15
Serapis 2-102
Seymour Admiral Sir Edward 2-70, **-157**
Seymour V-Admiral Beauchamp (later Lord Alcester) 2-135, **-147**
Shackleton, Sir Ernest 2-131
Shah **2-53,** -60
Shannon (1855) 1-140, -147
Shannon (1906) 2-49, -52
Shimonoseki, battle of 1-91, -135, **-142**
Shiré River, operations on 2-141, -148
Showing the flag **1-128, -130,** -132, **-134 /** 2-130, **-132, -134**
Sidon **1-155**
Sinope Bay, battle of 1-39
Skipjack **2-63**
Slavery, operations against **1-126, -127,** -129 / 2-103, -131, -133, **-140, -141**
Smith, Sir Francis Pettit 1-27
Society for Nautical Research 2-84
Spee, Admiral Graf von 2-58
Spider **2-63**
Starling 1-55, -152
Staunch 1-55
Stead, W T 2-29
Steam propulsion, development of 1-12, -14, -16, **-17, -19, -20, -21,** -24, **-25, -26,** -27, -29, **-34 /** 2-10, -19, **-46,** -49
Stopford, Admiral Sir Robert 1-57
Suez Canal 2-119
Sullivan, Sir Arthur 2-84
Sultan 1-106 / **2-23,** -99, -102, -106, **-144**
Sunny South **1-127**
Superb 2-30, **-144**
Surgeons 1-59, -60, **-69**
Sveaborg, bombardment of 1-143,

-144, **-154**
Swift **2-63,** -64
Symonds, Sir Wm 1-10, -11, -14

Taku Forts, bombardment of 2-156
Tarleton, Capt J **1-95**
TB 79 **2-108**
Temeraire 2-14, **-33, -34**
Terra Nova **2-139**
Terrible (1845) **1-18,** -24, -158
Terrible (1895) 2-52, -55, **-152**
Terror 1-131, **-139**
Theseus **2-65**
Thrush 2-109, -133
Thunderbolt 1-88
Thunderer (1872) 2-19, -22, **-26, -59,** -107
Thunderer (1911) **2-50**
Tiger **1-158**
Times, The 1-144 / 2-9, -119, -121
Topaze **1-22**
Trafalgar (1859) **1-156**
Trafalgar (1890) 2-33
Treaty of Paris 1856 1-146
Trewavas, Joseph, VC **1-89**
Tribune **1-119**
Trident 1-96
Troubridge, Capt Ernest 2-87, -88
Tryon, Admiral Sir George **2-6,** -70, -102, -161, -162, -164, -165, -167, **-170**
Tsushima, battle of 2-42, -87
Turrets 2-8, -9, -10, **-13, -14, -16,** -18, -20, **-26, -31, -32,** -33, -46

Undaunted 1-45
Underwater warfare: Destroyers **2-63,** -64; 'Infernal machines': **1-154;** Locomotive torpedoes 2-29, **-60,** -62; Rams 2-58, -59, **-166, -167;** Spar torpedoes **2-59;** Submarines **2-64,** -65; torpedo boats **2-60, -61,** -62, **-63,** -64, **-108;** Towed torpedoes 2-59

Valorous 2-100
Vanguard **2-48**
Vernon 2-60, **-61,** -62, -78

Victoria (1853) 1-11, -45
Victoria (1884) 2-30, -33, -162, -164, -165, -167, **-168, -170, -171**
Victoria and Albert I (1843 - renamed Osborne) 1-96, -97, **-98, -99, -102, -108, -109, -113, -116**
Victoria and Albert II (1855) **1-98, -99, -102,** -105, **-110, -117 / 2-104-105,** -110, **-114**
Victoria and Albert III (1899) **2-106,** -110, -113, **-114-115, -128**
Victoria, Princess **2-128**
Victoria, Queen 1-73, -74, -94, **-96, -97,** -99, -100, **-103, -105, -106, -108, -109, -110,** -113, -118, -199, / 2-29, -38, -99, -105, -106, -107, -110, -114, -118, **-120, -124, -126,** -161
Victory 1-10, -11, -87 / **2-64, -84**
Volage 2-10, **-74**
Von Tirpitz, Admiral 2-157

Warrior (1860) **1-30, -32, -33, -34,** -35, -42, -45, -46, **-48 /** 2-8, -19, -43, -48, -49, **-61**
Warspite (1807) **2-72**
Warspite (1884) 2-52
Watertight compartments 1-34, -42 / **2-163**
Watts, Sir Phillip 2-43, **-46,** -47, -54, -57
Weston, Dame Agnes **2-71,** -76
White, Sir Wm 2-26, -30, -33, **-38,** -39, -40, -43, -46, -49, **-52,** -53, -54, -121
Whitehead, Robert 2-29, -59, -62
Whiting 2-156
William IV 1-64, -92, **-93,** -97, -106, -108 / 2-103, -109
Wilson, A F Sir Arthur, VC 2-36, -60, -62, -64, -67, -149, -151, -152, -159, -162, -165, -167, -168, -172, **-173**
Wireless, naval 2-65, -67, -162
Worcester 1-70, **-80**
Wyllie, W L **2-37, -121**

Yenikale, capture of **1-159**

Zanzibar, bombardment of 2-51, -133, **-141**